BYGONE HERTFORDSHIRE

BYGONE HERTFORDSHIRE

EDITED BY WILLIAM ANDREWS

Republished by S.R. Publishers Ltd. 1969

First published by William Andrews & Co., Hull and London.
1898

BIBLIOGRAPHIC NOTE

illustrations which were in the body of the book appear at the end of the reprint.

© S.R. Publishers Ltd., East Ardsley, Wakefield, Yorkshire

S.B.N. 85409. 563. 2.

Printed in England by Kingprint Limited

Preface.

IN this volume I have tried, with the co-operation of local authors who have made a careful study of the annals of the county, to present in a popular and reliable form a series of studies of the more important and attractive chapters of Hertfordshire history.

If the book receives a similar welcome from the press and the public as that accorded to my previous productions I shall have reason to think that my labours have not been in vain.

WILLIAM ANDREWS.

THE HULL PRESS,
May 6th, 1898.

Contents.

Bygone Hertfordshire.

Historic Hertfordshire.

By Thomas Frost.

A CCORDING to the earliest accounts of the
geographical divisions of England, which
we owe to Roman writers, the county of Herts,
together with those of Bedford and Buckingham,
was inhabited at the time of the Roman subjugation of the island by a tribe whose name is
variously given as Catteuchlani, Cattidudani, and
Cattricludani. These names being British, their
signification is unknown, and the hap-hazard
guesses of archæologists who have endeavoured
to explain them may be disregarded. The
British town which was the capital of this tribe
at the time of the first Roman invasion is placed
by some writers on the site of the subsequent
Roman station of Verulamium, and by others at
Beech Bottom, one mile north of the present
town of St. Albans. Verulamium appears to

1

have been situated on the ridge which stretches from St. Michaels to St. Stephens, field-paths crossing the site.

Traces may still be found of the three admirable roads which were made by the Romans after the subjugation of the Britons. The Ermin Street entered the county at Northaw Common, from Enfield, in Middlesex, and thence by Newgate Street to Hertford. It then crossed the Lea to Porthill, beyond which it passed into Cambridgeshire. The Icknield Street entered from the west, crossing the boundary of the county a mile north of Tring, then passing through Ickleford, towards Baldock, and from Odsey Grange onward becoming the boundary between Hertfordshire and Cambridgeshire. The Watling Street entered the county at Elstree, near which was the Roman station of Sullonicæ, skirted St. Albans on the west, and passed through Redbourn into Bedfordshire.

Memorials of the Roman occupation have been found at many places. Verulamium was a very important town in those days, and Tacitus intimates that it was its wealth which prompted the Iceni, after sacking and burning London, to pass other military stations unmolested, in their eagerness to plunder the city on the Ver. It quickly recovered when the Roman power was again in the ascendant. In Stukeley's time the remains of the Roman wall, built of flints and red tiles, extended 1,760 yards from north to south, and one thousand from east to west. There are still in a field near the river two remnants of it, the longer only twenty yards, and rapidly crumbling away. It was in this town that Christianity was first preached to the Britons, and in 429 a synod was held here to take measures for the suppression of the heresy of Pelagius.

Camden writes, concerning St. Albans : "Were I to relate what common report affirms of the many Roman coins, statues of gold and silver, vessels, marble pillars, cornices, and wonderful monuments of ancient art, dug up here, I should scarcely be believed." In 1719 a Roman urn and other articles (engraved in Gough's edition of Camden) were discovered; and in 1767 a handsome vase of black pottery was turned up. At Wilbury Hill, near Baldock, is a square earthwork, six or seven acres in extent, which has been conjectured by some to have been a Roman amphitheatre, and by others a British or Roman fort. Roman coins have been found here, and in the neighbouring

villages of Newnham, Caldecott, and Hinxworth
many finds of Roman urns, coins, rings, beads, etc.,
have been made.   In 1802 four stone coffins were
disinterred in a field near Ware, and near them a
copper coin of Constantine.   About a mile from
Hinxworth a Roman earthwork can still be dis-
tinctly traced.

Near Hexton traces of a camp exist, which some
antiquaries regard as a Roman work, because
Roman relics have been found there ; but others
contend that it is Danish.   Remains of a Roman
villa were found a few years ago in a field near
Purwell Mill, on the road from Hitchin to Stevenage.   Roman trinkets were found about a hundred
years ago at Braughing, on the road from
Ware to Royston ; and about the middle of the
last century an interesting find of Roman pottery
was made at Westmill, near Buntingford.

The withdrawal of the Romans, and the coming
of the Saxons, checked for a time the progress of
civilisation and prosperity in the county.   St.
Albans was plundered and burned by the new
comers, and it did not recover from the spoliation
until the erection of the abbey by Offa, King of
Mercia, in 791.   Under the Heptarchy, a small
portion of the county was included in the kingdom

of Essex, the boundary commencing southward, according to Salmon, at a bank in the parish of Cheshunt, " which anciently reached from Middlesex, through Theobald's Park, across Goffe's Lane, to Thunderfield Grove, over Beaumont Green, to Nine Acres Wood." He adds that there was a custom in the manor of Cheshunt, " by which the eldest brother inherits above the bank, and the youngest below it, in the same fields, which could not have been introduced but from the different laws of a different government." The boundary between the two kingdoms was continued northward along the line of the Ermin Street.

In the course of the tenth century the county suffered, on several occasions, from the incursions of the Danes, a body of whom, in 950, plundered the abbey of St. Albans and carried off some of the bones of the saint, which are said, however, to have been subsequently restored. St. Albans suffered much more severely from the Norman conquest, in consequence of the opposition of the abbot to the progress of the Conqueror. William crossed the Thames at Wallingford, and had reached Berkhampsted, when he found the road along which he was triumphantly marching bar-

ricaded by trees, which the abbot of St. Albans
had caused to be cut down and thrown across it.
By this means time was gained for the nobles of
the county to be convened at St. Albans, for the
purpose of consulting as to the means to be adopted
to check the Norman advance, and, if possible,
to save the country from a foreign domination.
Nothing in that direction could be accomplished,
however, and William continued his march. The
abbot sought refuge in the monastery of Ely, and
the Conqueror revenged the unsuccessful attempt
to stay his progress by seizing all the lands of the
abbey of St. Albans between Barnet and London,
together with the manor of Redbourn. Only the
interposition of Archbishop Lanfranc saved the
abbey from complete ruin.

During the conflict between John and the
barons the strong places of the county changed
owners on more than one occasion. Hertford
Castle, which was held by the King, was taken,
after a stout defence, by the baronial army,
supported by a French force, under the command
of the Dauphin, the eldest son of Philip II., King
of France. Berkhampsted Castle held out against
the foreigners until John sent an order for its
surrender. The less important castle of Bishop's

Stortford (which derives its name from having formerly belonged to the bishopric of London) was demolished by order of John, in revenge for the bishop having joined with the bishops of Ely and Worcester in publishing the Papal interdict. The King came badly out of the struggle with the Pope, and found it necessary to give his own manor of Guildford to the bishop, by way of compensation for the destruction of the castle. "The castle hill," says Salmon, "stands yet a monument of King John's power and revenge; and the bishop's lands remain a monument of the Pope's entire victory over him."

In 1264 St. Albans was a scene of great tumult and disorder, which arose out of a dispute between the abbot and the townsmen, concerning the use of the abbey mills. In the midst of the confusion thus occasioned, the Queen, Eleanor of Provence, arrived on a visit to the abbey, and found the way crowded by the inhabitants, who hoped to obtain the royal intercession in behalf of their cause. In this aim they were foiled by the abbot causing the Queen to be introduced into the monastery by some private way; and this so enraged the inhabitants that they barricaded every avenue to the town, and seized and decapitated the constable

of Hertford Castle and his three attendants.
For this outrage the King fined the town one
hundred marks, which was promptly paid, the
inhabitants being probably glad, when they
became calmer, to escape so well.

The peace of the country was not again
disturbed until the reign of Richard II., when the
blow struck by Walter Hilliard, commonly called
Wat Tyler, at Dartford, found an echo in the
breasts of the serfs of Hertfordshire. In the
neighbourhood of St. Albans they rose in great
force, and made a threatening demonstration
against the abbey, reiterating the demands of the
insurgents encamped on Blackheath. Thomas
Delamare, the then abbot, conceded their
demands, in order to save the abbey from
destruction ; but the insurrection was no sooner
suppressed than the king issued a proclamation
commanding that all persons, bond or free, who
owed service to the abbot, should perform the
same as before, under a penalty of forfeiture " of
all they had to lose," besides such other punish-
ments as they might have rendered themselves
liable to suffer. Having taken measures for the
prompt punishment of as many of the insurgents
of Kent and Essex as had been captured,

Richard set out for St. Albans, accompanied by his stern chief justice, Sir Robert Tresillian, and escorted by a body of one thousand soldiers. The trial of the men who had been most active in the rising, and had the ill-fortune to be captured, resulted in the hanging of fifteen—some writers say eighteen—of them ; and all the commons of the county, between the ages of fifteen and sixty, were summoned to attend in the great court of the abbey, and make oath to behave as faithful subjects of the king, and never more disturb the public peace.

During the sanguinary civil war between the partisans of the elder branch of the Plantagenet dynasty and those of the usurping Lancastrian faction, three of the most important battles were fought within the limits of this county. The day on which the first battle at St. Albans was fought, the 22nd of May, 1455, found the Lancastrians, under the reigning king, Henry VI., in possession of the town, upon which the Yorkists advanced from two sides, St. Peter's on the north, and Key Field, near the Sopwell nunnery, on the south. The engagement lasted scarcely an hour, but it proved disastrous, for the time, to the Lancastrian cause. The king, who had set up his standard in St. Peter's Street, was wounded in the neck by an arrow, towards the close of the battle, and on the retreat of his troops, who left him alone under the royal banner, he took refuge in a baker's shop. On the victorious Yorkists entering the town, he was visited there by the Duke of York, who conducted him to his apartments in the abbey, whence he was removed on the following day to London, and became a prisoner in the Tower.

Four years later, Henry having gained his liberty under a compact by which the Duke of York was to succeed him on the throne, he and Queen Margaret visited St. Albans, where they were sumptuously entertained at the monastery by Abbot Wheathampstead. This visit was repeated in the same year, and in 1461 under more exciting circumstances. The Civil War had then been renewed, in consequence of the opposition of the Queen to an arrangement which would have excluded her own son from the throne. On the 17th of February, the Yorkists being then in possession of the town, they were attacked by a stronger Lancastrian force, and driven back upon the Market Place, where, as night was coming on, they were thrown into

disorder, a precipitate flight commenced. Henry,
who was again a captive, was left behind with
Lord Montague, his chamberlain, and two or
three attendants. On this becoming known to
the Queen, she hastened, accompanied by her
son, Prince Edward, to join him; and the royal
party, attended by the nobles of their party,
proceeded to the abbey, at the doors of which
they were met by the abbot and the monks,
chanting hymns of thanksgiving and triumph for
the King's safety, and his restoration to liberty.
A procession was then formed to the high altar,
where a thanksgiving service was held, followed
by another at the shrine of St. Alban. The
royal party were then conducted to the apartments
prepared for them in the monastery. The town
was, during these religious observances, being
plundered by the Lancastrian soldiery. The
royal party remained at St. Albans several days,
when, learning that the Duke of York was
approaching the town by forced marches, they
withdrew to a safer place. The nobles who fell
in the battle were interred in the church of St.
Peters, from which their monuments were
removed when the chancel was demolished, early
in the last century.

In 1471, when the battle of Barnet was fought, the famous Earl of Warwick, who had controlled the destinies of both factions in a great measure throughout this long and sanguinary struggle, had changed sides, and now commanded the forces of the Lancastrian party. These had taken up a position on Gladsmuir Heath, a short distance north of Hadley, which has now approached closely to Barnet; and there the engagement commenced at an early hour on a misty morning in April, and was continued in a most obstinate manner until the hopes of Queen Margaret and her adherents were extinguished by the death of Warwick and a great slaughter of his troops. This result of the battle practically gave the balance to the Yorkists, the subsequent fight at Tewkesbury being the final and almost despairing effort of the Lancastrians. At the point where the road northward divided towards St. Albans and Hatfield, and which, according to tradition, is the spot where Warwick fell, an obelisk was erected in 1740 by Sir Jeremy Sambrook, to commemorate the event, the inscription on it merely recording the bare fact and the date.

It was stated by Lord Lytton, in the address with which he opened the congress of the British

Archæological Association in 1866, when it was held at St. Albans, that on the summit of the tower of Hadley Church there was still to be seen the lantern which, according to tradition, lighted the forces of Edward IV. in their advance through the dense mist which prevailed on the morning of the battle, and which was believed to have been raised by the incantations of the supposed necromancer, Friar Bungay. Through the veil of that mist, said Lord Lytton, the battle was fought which extinguished the power of the great feudal lords, and inaugurated a new era in the records of freedom and civil progress. But as Friar Bungay was the contemporary of Roger Bacon, who died in 1284, the tradition of the time must be very far wrong in ascribing the mist of Easter Monday, 1471, to his magic powers.

The changes in ecclesiastical matters which were made in the next century, and which were prepared for by the victories of the Yorkists over the adherents of the persecuting house of Lancaster, increased the social and political effects of the transfers of estates which were brought about by the vicissitudes of the protracted Civil War. On the 5th of December, 1539, Sir Thomas Pope, one of the Commissioners of Henry VIII.

for the suppression of monastic institutions, received the surrender of St. Alban's Abbey, with all its privileges and possessions, from Abbot Boreman; and the results to accrue from it were soon made apparent. All the monastic buildings were demolished in the course of this and the following reign; but the church was saved from impending destruction by the exertions of the inhabitants, who, in 1553, in the reign of Edward VI., purchased it from the royal commissioners for the nominal sum of four hundred pounds, and made it parochial. The land and buildings of the Benedictine Convent at Sopwell, about half a mile from St. Albans, were granted to Sir Richard Lee. The abbey lands in the manor of Cashiobury, which seems to have included the whole of the parish of Watford, were conveyed to Richard Morison, who was employed by Henry VIII. and Edward VI. in several embassies to continental courts.

In a great measure Hertfordshire was spared participation in the troubles that befell the kingdom through the attempts of Charles I. to make the prerogatives of the Crown override the constitutional powers of the House of Commons and the liberties of the people. This happy immunity was due, in some degree, to the fact that the castles and embattled mansions of the county were, for the most part, already in ruins when the armies of the King and the Parliament were set in motion against each other. The castle of Berkhampsted had been long uninhabited, and even in Leland's time was " much in ruin." The castle of Bishop's Stortford had been in ruins since the reign of John. These circumstances go far to account for the fact that the chief event of the Civil War, so far as this county was concerned, was the march of Cromwell from Cambridge to St. Albans, and that was made near the end of the war.

The story of the Rye House Plot, which was the chief incident in the history of the county in the latter half of the seventeenth century, is told in another part of this volume. In the quieter and happier times in which we now live, history of a better kind is made by the association with the county of statesmen like Lords Melbourne and Palmerston, men, in the words of the late Lord Lytton, " akin by family connexion, akin still more by the English attributes they had in common—an exquisite geniality of temper, united with a robust and simple manliness of character."

The Only Roman Theatre in Great Britain.

By Charles Henry Ashdown, f.r.g.s.

UPON the southern slope of the gentle valley of the Ver, and facing the ancient town of St. Albans, clustering around its monastic nucleus the venerable Abbey, lie great masses of ancient masonry, the thin red tiles in which sufficiently indicate its Roman origin. These remains, together with a deep fosse and a causeway across the valley, are almost the only relics we now possess to indicate the site of the great Roman city of Verulamium, itself an immediate successor of the far-spreading British capital of the Cassii, and the home of Cymbeline and Cassivelaunus. Great Cæsar and his legions trod this classic site, the farthest north of his second invasion, but a century elapsed after the death of the Conqueror ere the cry of the centurion was again heard within the ringed enclosure. Then Rome came to stay. The wattled skin-covered defences of the British city gave place to a high and broad rampart, composed of the native flint embedded in a matrix of that mortar which the Romans knew so well how to make, and whose adamantine hardness evokes our admiration at the present day, while layers of broad tiles strengthened the erection at regular intervals. Wide streets, running at right angles to each other, intersected the site, temples and public and private buildings appeared, and a large measure of prosperity was pouring upon the city through the great influx of foreign traders and Roman immigrants of all grades, when dire destruction, sack, and ruin fell upon the community like a thunderbolt during the Boadicean revolt in A.D. 61. The major portion of the eighty thousand victims of the insurrection perished in or near Verulamium, which became a wasted and blackened ruin.

But, like a phœnix from its ashes, the city rose again, and in a style of magnificence far excelling its previous appearance. The spacious streets were lined with luxurious villas, replete with the objects of art and culture obtaining in ancient Rome; the Forum, Basilica, and great public baths lay in the heart of the city, where also the frescoed Greek Theatre delighted many a gaily-dressed audience, while without the city walls the Amphitheatre and the spacious lake attracted

2

crowds of light-hearted citizens. For four centuries, Verulamium, the capital of Southern Britain and sharing with York in the honour of being a *municipium*, flourished under the smiles of successive emperors, until the time arrived when the legionaries were summoned home to defend the heart of the empire from barbarian invaders, and the Britons were left to the mercies of marauding Saxons and plundering Danes. For years the city was the centre of contention and strife, and finally was completely destroyed by fire about a century after the cessation of the Roman occupation. For three hundred years the ruins lay undisturbed and desolate, but when St. Alban's Monastery was founded by King Offa of Mercia (755 to 794), the devastated city was used as a quarry for building materials, and enormous quantities of Roman tiles, stone, and flint were removed in order to form that magnificent pile of buildings which reared their massive fronts upon the opposite slope of the valley, and crowned Holmhurst Hill with masses of solid masonry, some of which have remained to the present day to challenge our admiration and awe.

The site of Verulamium has for many years been used for agricultural purposes; the plough, that great leveller of man's handiwork, removes slowly but surely the remaining traces of the past, and buries under one monotonous layer of earth sculptured stone and chiselled column, carved cornice and frescoed panel.   From time to time interesting discoveries are made upon the site of the ruined city, but probably the most important one of the present century is that of the Theatre, which holds the unique distinction of being the only building of that nature as yet discovered in Great Britain.   Of amphitheatres there are a number in existence in or near the sites of former Roman cities or stations, but this is the only erection, so far as is known at present, which was exclusively devoted to dramatic representations.

About fifty years ago an archæologist, while searching for remains upon the site of Verulam, came upon a small portion of masonry imbedded in the bank upon the north side of the drive to Gorhambury, the historic seat of the great Sir Francis Bacon, Lord Verulam and Viscount St. Albans.   The scene of the discovery is about one hundred yards from the entrance-lodge, and about twice that distance from the old Saxon Church of St. Michael, the Shrine of Baconians, wherein the great philosopher is buried.   Investigations proved that but a small portion of masonry existed upon the north side of the road, but upon the south side the indications were found to be more promising.　Excavations were at once commenced and followed up with vigour, and gradually the superincumbent earth was removed and the subject of this paper was laid bare.

The earliest theatres of which we have any knowledge were those of the Greeks ; the outer walls contained a little more than a semicircle, and there was an inner concentric circle, the diameter of which was one-third that of the theatre.　The area inclosed by the inner circle was devoted to the chorus, and was called the orchestra,—all exhibitions of dancing occurred within this space. The width of the stage was always in fixed proportion to the size of the orchestra, being twice its diameter, the depth of the stage being one-seventh of that measurement.

Roman theatres were modelled upon those of Greece ; the orchestra, however, was much smaller, as the chorus did not occupy such an important position, and this space was chiefly utilised for seating spectators of the highest rank.　The outer walls rarely exceeded a semicircle, and the stage was much larger than in the Greek theatre, being twice the diameter of the orchestra in length, and one-fourth in depth, in order to afford accommodation for the chorus.   A corridor ran round every ancient Greek and Roman theatre, forming a space between the massive outer wall and a thinner concentric inner wall, and over this passage the seats for the ladies were invariably placed.   Below these positions of honour, and ranging downwards to the barrier of the orchestra, occurred the rows of benches for ordinary spectators, who sat upon one seat and placed their feet upon the one next below them.   Dressing-rooms were built at the sides of the stage ; the scenery occupied the back of the stage only, and no wings were used, otherwise it was similar to that obtaining in the modern theatre, and represented interiors and exteriors as the nature of the play required, being changed when necessary.   Behind the backcloth was the "Chamber of Horrors," a small compartment wherein murders and tragic deeds generally were supposed to occur.

It may be interesting to many readers to compare the Theatre thus disclosed with that which has been revealed at Pompeii, with which they may possibly be familiar.   The similarity is remarkable, both as regards configuration and

distribution of parts. The Theatre at Verulamium
is one hundred and ninety feet three inches in
diameter, that at Pompeii one hundred and ninety-
five feet. Both have their outer walls built upon
the plan of the Greek theatre, comprising 240°,
while the internal measurements of the one may
be taken as being almost identical with the other.
The corridor between the outer walls at Verulamium is nine feet wide ; the stage is forty-six feet
long, and eight feet nine inches deep. A dressing-
room at the eastern (or right hand) side of the
stage has a crude tesselated pavement with no
pattern, the tesseræ being composed of pieces of
Roman tile about one inch square, lying upon a
thin layer of concrete. Although excavations
were carried out upon the western side of the
stage, no corresponding room was discovered.
With respect to the thickness of the walls, the
outer one is five feet ten inches, the next three
feet six inches, the *scena,* or wall behind the stage,
two feet six inches, and all the remainder two
feet. The entrances into the orchestra appear to
be three in number, although only two, one
opposite the centre of the stage, and another on
the east side, have as yet been discovered. The
space over the corridor, appropriated by the

ladies, is twelve feet wide, and the distance from
thence to the boundary wall of the orchestra is
thirty-three feet six inches.   Indications of a wall
were found within the precincts of the orchestra,
and at but a small distance from the boundary
wall ; it probably afforded a space for a specially-
privileged portion of the Roman community.

Great care seems to have been expended upon
the interior decoration of the Verulamium Theatre,
the whole surface apparently having been ornamented with frescoes.   The method of application
appears to have been that in general use, namely,
the affixing of a thick coating of mortar, which
was reduced to a uniform even surface in order
to receive a thin layer of very fine and perfectly
white plaster.   Upon the latter, and while both of
the layers were wet, mineral water-colours were
laid, which adhered to and dried with it.   Being
native colours and free from artificial admixtures,
the frescoes discovered were in an excellent state
of preservation, being almost as bright as when
first laid on, while the *intonaco*, or thin finishing
coat of plaster, still retained its original smooth-
ness.   The colours used were generally of a
cream or white tone, with brown, red, and blue
stripes ; traces of flower painting also occurred.

Slabs of marble, thirteen-sixteenths of an inch in thickness, were freely used in the decorations of the Theatre, the marble being similar to that used in lining the basin of the fountain at the well-known Roman Villa at Bignor, Sussex.*

The fact that the Theatre at Verulamium is constructed upon the Greek model may be taken as a conclusive proof that the building is of great antiquity, and, in fact, be contemporaneous with the rebuilding of the city after its destruction by Queen Boadicea, inasmuch as we find that theatres upon the Roman plan were introduced a few years before the birth of our Lord, and spread through the great Empire to its remotest parts. Thus the architect who planned the place of amusement at Verulamium must have been one of the old school to whom the innovation was entirely unknown, or else so imperfectly understood that he did not care to put it into practice.

It is a matter for comment that the famous " School of Historians" of the Monastery of St. Alban make no mention of this building in their multitudinous mass of local notes and allusions, although one historiographer, Roger de Wendover,

* A very crude drawing of the excavations, as they appeared in 1847, is extant, and this has been copied to illustrate " St. Albans : Historical and Picturesque," by the same author.

may or may not refer to it in a vaguely-worded story of a vision vouchsafed to him. This absence of allusion may be due to the Theatre having been partially demolished previous to the establishment of the "School," and probably in the time of Ealdred and Eadmer, the eighth and ninth Abbots of the Monastery. These Abbots are said by Matthew Paris to have carried out extensive excavations and researches in the ruins of Veru-lamium, where the remains of many palaces, temples, etc., were destroyed in order to obtain building materials for carrying on the necessary additions to the flourishing Monastery over which they had the rule. In all probability the Theatre was one of the ruined "temples" mentioned, and the stones which vibrated with the plaudits of excited multitudes over eighteen centuries ago, may since have thrilled with the harmony of the Romish Mass, and now listen quiescently to the sweet voice of the singer within the venerable walls of St. Alban's Abbey.

After the first excavation of the Theatre the earth was replaced, but upon the visit of the British Archæological Association to St. Albans in 1869, the building was once more uncovered, though not to such an extent as before. At the

termination of the congress, the ruins were once
more hidden from the light of day, and from that
time to this successive crops of succulent turnips
have flourished uninterruptedly over the classic
site of the only Roman Theatre in Great Britain.

St. Alban's Abbey.

By England Howlett.

IN the days of the Roman occupation of England, the City of Verulamium, situate on the bank of the little river Ver, was one of great importance. It was during the persecution of the Christians under Diocletian (A.D. 300-305) that a Roman called Albanus suffered martyrdom, and became, indeed, the Protomartyr of Britain. The story, as told by Bede,* is as follows :—Albanus, still a pagan, received and sheltered in his cottage a certain Christian priest, who was hiding himself from persecution. The sight of his constant prayers and vigils greatly struck Albanus. He sought instruction from his visitor, accepted his teaching, and speedily became himself a Christian. The place of refuge of the priest was by some means discovered, and when the Roman soldiers appeared at his door, Albanus presented himself instead of his guest and teacher, wrapped in the priest's long cloak. He was led before the judge,

* *Hist.* Eccles.

who was at that moment assisting at a great
sacrifice, and was told that because he had concealed
and had procured the escape of a "sacrilegious
despiser of the Gods" he should take the place of
the priest, and should suffer the punishment justly
due to him, if it appeared that his own ancient faith
had been in anyway shaken. Albanus, giving his
name to the judge, professed himself a Christian,
refused to sacrifice to the Gods, and was then
severely scourged. But nothing could shake him,
and an order was given for his immediate beheading. Accordingly, he was led from the city
toward a hill which rose on the opposite side of
the Ver. The bridge which crossed the river was
narrow, and there was so great a crowd seeking to
pass, and to witness the execution, that Albanus,
eager for martyrdom, feared that evening would
come before he could reach the appointed place.
But at his prayer the stream shrank away and the
host of witnesses was able to pass over dryshod.
The executioner was so impressed by the miracle
that he flung away his sword, and fell at the feet
of the martyr, desiring rather to die with him than
to take his life. The hill was at last reached; and
on its summit Albanus, thirsting, desired water
from God. Immediately a spring burst forth,

which, when its ministry had been performed, returned again into the heart of the earth. Then the martyr's head was stricken off, but the executioner who had taken the place of him who had refused to strike the blow was not permitted to rejoice in his evil deed; his eyes fell on the earth at the same moment that the head of Albanus struck it, the other was beheaded at the same time and place. The judge, continues Bede, impressed by so many miraculous signs, soon discontinued the persecution of the Christians.

A few years after the martyrdom of Albanus, a church was raised in his honour on the site where he died. We learn, from Bede, that this church was worthy of the saint whom it commemorated; and that frequent miracles—healing of the sick, and other signs—took place in it. Before the end of the eighth century, this church appears to have been reduced to ruins, and the actual place of burial of the Saint unknown.

About the year 793, Offa, King of Mercia, founded a monastery in honour of Albanus, and procured his canonization from the Pope Adrian. It seems that no one knew where the relics of the protomartyr lay. A vision was, however, vouchsafed to Offa at Bath, and, guided by a miraculous

light, the coffin which contained the remains was
duly found by the King. These remains were
placed in a reliquary, and conveyed to the small
temporary church which had been prepared for
them, until that of the new monastery should be
built. The monastery was at once founded, and
a company of Benedictines was established in it.
Thus arose that great Abbey of St. Alban, which
was to be distinguished by so many privileges,
and by such enormous donations, and which, from
its foundation to its dissolution, was generally
regarded as the principal home of the Benedictine.
Order in England.

Thirteen abbots ruled the monastery from the
foundation of it by Offa to the Norman Conquest,
and many of these were of royal descent, a
sufficient indication of the great distinction at
once assigned to the house of St. Alban.

It was at this time that the town began to
gather round the walls of the Abbey; and it is
said that the sixth Abbot, by name Ulsi, founded
the three churches, which were dedicated to St.
Peter, St. Michael, and St. Stephen. The twelfth
Abbot, Ealdred, set to work deliberately to break
up the buildings which formed the ancient city of
Verulamium, which had gradually become the

THE TOWER, ST. ALBAN'S ABBEY. (BEFORE RESTORATION.)

resort of men and women of evil repute, and robbers from the neighbouring forests. The materials from the old city were carefully set aside for the purpose of building the new church.

In the year 1077, when Paul of Caen became Abbot of the Monastery, the church which was built by Offa of Mercia in the year 793, was still standing. Abbot Paul pulled down the Saxon Church, but much of the material—together with the stones and tiles from Verulamium—went to build the new church, which was completed in eleven years, "the vastest and sternest structure of his age."* The Roman tiles from the demolished city which are so largely used in this church, give, what Freeman terms, the effect of *sternness.* Similar tiles are used in the village church at Brixworth, in Northamptonshire, and in others where an old Roman station was at hand for the builders at the time. Nowhere, however, are these tiles so extensively employed as at St. Albans.

This Norman church appears to have been dedicated in the year 1115, during the abbacy of Richard d'Aubeny, who was the successor of Paul of Caen. At the dedication, King Henry I. and

* E. A. Freeman. "Norm. Conq."

his Queen were present, and there was a tremendous concourse of nobles, bishops, and abbots, and it is said that the whole company remained feasting at St. Albans for some time.

Of this church there now remains the tower, transepts, and the eastern portion of the nave. When originally built the transepts opened eastward into two apsidal chapels, and the west front was flanked by two square towers.

The church appears to have remained unaltered until the abbacy of John de Cella (1195-1214). Now, at this time, one of our greatest architectural developments had taken place, and the light and graceful Early English style replaced the sometimes rude, and always stern work of the Norman period. Abbot John appears to have been an enthusiastic builder, and he undertook to rebuild the western front of the church in the then new Early English style ; indeed, it is said, he intended rebuilding the whole of the nave, and was only prevented from so doing by want of funds to carry out the work. William of Trumpington (1215-1235) carried on the work of his predecessor, and he rebuilt at the western end of the nave four piers with their arches, on the south side, and three piers with their arches, on the north side.

It was in the year 1256 that the next great architectural work was undertaken, and then it was at the eastern end of the church. The convent determined to rebuild the presbytery, the short Norman one was no doubt insufficient for the growing requirements of the ecclesiastics, but the new plan involved a complete alteration of the original Norman design. The apse was removed entirely, and the building was continued eastward for a considerable distance.

Further eastward, although rather narrowed in width, there was added the Lady Chapel, which consists of three bays, and is square ended. This work brought the ground plan of this magnificent church to completion. It is, however, evident that the work at the east end extended over a considerable number of years, probably from 1256 to 1300. The Lady Chapel is a beautiful specimen of the Decorated Period of our architecture, and is as perfect in art as anything which its age furnished.

The effect produced by the extreme unbroken length of the nave at St. Alban's has led to the very general assertion that the Great Church at St. Alban's Monastery is the longest in England, and consequently in the world, with of course the exception of St. Peter's at Rome. But careful measurements have shown that this is an error, and that Winchester Cathedral is the longest of our mediæval churches.

During the succeeding years, when the Perpendicular style had taken the place of the Decorated, a good many changes were effected in the building. The walls of the nave-aisles were lowered, and the roofs were flattened. Perpendicular windows were also inserted at the western end and in the transept fronts. After the dissolution of the abbey, great havoc was wrought, and much of the delicate work in the interior either totally destroyed or greatly injured.

The church remained in the hands of the Crown until the year 1553, and then the main body of it was granted for £400 to the mayor and burgesses to be the parish church, and they were also empowered to establish a Grammar School within the ancient Lady-chapel. To effect these alterations the arches at the east end of the feretory, and the aisles in a line with them, were walled up. East of this wall an open passage was formed quite through the church, so as to allow of an independent approach to the Lady-

THE CHOIR, LOOKING EAST, ST. ALBAN'S ABBEY.

chapel, which then became the Grammar School, and so continued for a great number of years.

The nave was once rich in brasses and monuments, but most of these have long since disappeared. The memorial of Sir John Mandeville, the famous traveller, is against the second pier from the west on the north side of the nave. The inscription runs as follows :—

"Siste gradum properans, requiescit Mandevil urnâ
    Hic humili ; norunt et monumenta mori."

"Lo in this Inn of Travellers doth lie
  One rich in nothing but in memory ;
  His name was Sir John Mandeville ; content,
  Having seen much, with a final continent
  Towards which he travelled ever since his birth
  And at last pawned his body for yt earth
  Which by a Statute must in mortgage be
  Till a Redeemer come to set it free."

The screen which divides the nave from the choir of the monks is known as the Screen or Chapel of St. Cuthbert. It is a magnificent piece of late Decorated work. At one time it, no doubt, crossed both aisles, and thus completely shut off the eastern portion of the church.

The great feature of interest in the south transept is the introduction of the baluster shafts, which appear in the arches of the triforium on the eastern side. These shafts doubtless belonged to the Saxon church of Offa, and were worked up with other material into the new church.

The roofs of both the transepts and the nave are flat, and appear to represent Norman construction of somewhat late date. The vaulting of the choir, the Lady-chapel, and south aisle is quadripartite.

The reredos, which separates the presbytery from the retrochoir, was the work of Abbot Wallingford (1476-1484). There is a door on either side, opening to the great Shrine of St. Alban at the back. The whole screen is most elaborate in design and workmanship, and the unusual height to which it is carried renders it a most conspicuous and stately object in the church.

The Shrine of St. Alban occupied the centre of the chapel. A portal on each side opened to the north and south aisles; this was in accordance with the usual arrangements by which pilgrims and worshippers were enabled to enter by one portal, pass in front of the shrine, and so leave the chapel by the opposite portal. On the north side, in the easternmost bay, is the Watching Chamber, which was always to be found in close proximity to a wealthy shrine, such as that of St.

Alban. The Watching Chamber was left when the shrine was carried off, and still remains. The base of the shrine was discovered when some restoration work was in progress about twenty years ago. This base would appear to belong to the Early Decorated period, and before its ruthless mutilation must have been an exquisite piece of workmanship. At the west end the pediment shows the beheading of St. Alban, the head of the Martyr having just fallen to the ground. At the east end the scourging of the Saint is represented, and below is the figure of a king, holding in his left hand a cruciform church. This is Offa, the founder of the Abbey.

The Watching Chamber is a wooden structure. The upper portion projects and resembles a gallery, with an open arcade, looking into the church. The lower part of this structure contains almeries or lockers, in which reliquaries and sacred vessels were kept, a steep wooden staircase leading to the upper chamber or gallery. The whole is of rather late Perpendicular date.

In the bay opposite to the Watching Chamber is the chantry tomb of Humphrey, Duke of Gloucester, fourth and youngest son of King Henry IV. Duke Humphrey was arrested during the Parliament held at Bury St. Edmund's in the year 1446, and was found a few days afterwards dead in his bed, murdered, it is believed, by order of Queen Margaret. His body was taken to St. Albans, and the monument, which had previously been prepared, raised over it. Nearly two hundred years ago the vault below the monument was opened, when the body of the unfortunate duke was found entire. Strange to say, the opening to the vault was left in an insecure condition, and great desecration of the remains in the carrying away of bones continued until the late restoration, when the vault was secured. Before the discovery of the body, the notion prevailed that the duke was buried in the old Cathedral of St. Paul's, in London, and that the tomb of Sir John Beauchamp was his, and this gave rise to the proverb of "dining with Duke Humphrey." A custom prevailed of strewing herbs before the monument in the Cathedral, and sprinkling them with water and men who strolled about in "Paul's walk," in the Cathedral, in want of a dinner, were familiar enough with this tomb, and were said to "dine with Duke Humphrey."

In the centre of the Lady Chapel, after the first battle of St. Albans (May 23, 1455), were

ST. ALBAN'S SHRINE.

buried three great Lancastrian nobles who fell during this battle. These were Edmund Beaufort, Duke of Somerset; Henry Percy, Earl of Northumberland; and the Lord Clifford. They were all killed in the street, near to St. Peter's Church : and no one dared to touch or remove their bodies, until the Abbot of St. Albans, after considerable difficulty, obtained leave from the victorious Duke of York to bury them in the church. They were buried in the order of their rank, the duke lying furthest to the east.

The walls of both the Lady Chapel and antechapel are constructed largely of Roman tile, procured in part no doubt from the demolished apse, and thinly coated externally with flint work. Tiles are indeed used more or less in all the later building throughout the church.

The Cloisters occupied a large space on the south side of the nave. Of this great Cloister— probably about 150 feet square, and the very centre of monastic life,—nothing whatever remains. The refectory was on the south side, and the dormitory on the east. The Chapter House intervened between the dormitory and the transept. From the foundations it is evident it was a long parallelogram, with an apsidal termination.

In this Chapter House were buried many of the earlier abbots, including Paul of Caen (the builder of the Norman church), John of Cella, and William of Trumpington.

Nicholas Breakspeare, a candidate for admission to St. Alban's Monastery, was eventually raised to the chair of St. Peter at Rome, under the title of Pope Adrian IV., and he is the only Englishman who has ever attained to this dignity. Gorham, the eighteenth abbot of the Abbey (1151), received from Pope Adrian peculiar privileges for the Abbey and monastery, and which were allowed to no other throughout the country. From this time the abbot and his successors assumed the mitre.

It seems somewhat strange that the monastic buildings have disappeared more completely at St. Albans than around any other great English monastery. There is not much left to tell of the early life of the Benedictines, to whom the church belonged, and who served and worshipped at its altars. An especial set of chambers was provided for the use of the King whenever he should halt at St. Albans; and after each battle of St. Albans Henry VI. was brought by the victors to these chambers, having first been allowed to kneel in the church before the great shrine. Of all this grand pile of buildings, which at one time covered the whole hill on the south side of the church, and stretched down to the river, nothing whatever remains. The whole of the monastic buildings, with the ground lying round about the church, were granted to Sir Richard Lee in 1540. He at once began the work of destruction, and carried it out so completely that now the great gateway, which stands somewhat below the west front of the church, is the sole remaining relic of the monastery.

Forty abbots ruled St. Albans from its foundation to the Dissolution. Of these abbots, Willegod was the first, and Richard Boreman de Stevenache the last. He was in reality chosen by the royal interest, and put in to execute the instructions of the King and Parliament with a good grace. He surrendered the Abbey on the 5th December, 1539, and delivered the conventual seal to the visitors appointed by the Crown. This seal, which is of ivory, is now in the British Museum.

The King assigned to Boreman a yearly pension of £266 13s. 4d., and various allowances to the monks of the Abbey. The abbot and twenty of these monks were surviving when Queen Mary came to the throne in 1553.

The rich possessions of the monastery were dispersed among the interested courtiers, who had so willingly favoured the King's views, and quickly a scene of desolation and desecration followed.

Cardinal Wolsey was the thirty-eighth Abbot of St. Albans, and he took it in commendam. This was such a violation of the canon law, and such an invasion of the rule and government in which abbeys had been held, that it seemed to portend some fatal blow to the monastic institutions.

There is no record remaining that Wolsey ever came down to take possession ; nor of any act done by him with reference to this monastery during his commendamship, which lasted until his downfall, except a gift of plate to the monastery, and the following presentation in right of his abbacy :—" I find William Wakefield inducted into the vicarage of St. Peter's, in the town of St. Albans, by virtue of the letters of Thomas, Lord Cardinal and Archishop of York and Abbot of St. Albans."*

In thus giving an outline of the history of the Abbey of St. Albans, it seems wise to stop short at the dissolution of the monastery. Evil days

---

* Cole MS., Brit. Mus.

then fell on this noble pile of buildings. Destroying hands plundered and ruined wantonly, until much magnificent architectural work has been lost to us for ever.

Of late years a great work of restoration has been carried on, and it may safely be asserted that no work has ever called forth such fierce controversy. It must be left for posterity to pronounce judgment on this restoration. In the present day, opinion is much divided on the subject; but when time shall have obliterated all prejudice, the recent work will then stand forth for what it is really worth.

The Abbots' Claims and Albanians' Grievances.

Hertfordshire in the Peasants' Revolt.

By W. R. Willis.

THE county of Hertford, and the town of St. Albans in particular, participated in no small degree in the social disorders of the thirteenth and fourteenth centuries, which culminated in the civil wars, and the ultimate abolition of serfdom. It may be interesting to recall some features of the national history as it worked itself out in the county of Hertford. In common with the peasantry throughout the country, the Hertfordshire villans were in serfdom, but the position of the men of St. Albans was slightly different in some respects to that of their fellows in the country, although the essential features were similar. In the Domesday Survey the town and burgesses of St. Albans are mentioned as part of the possessions of " the Abbot and Convent of St. Albans, who held it of the King *in capite*," and is said to contain at the time forty-six burgesses, who were the " demesne men of the Abbot."

It is the attempt of the townsmen to assert their freedom from the rule of the Abbot as lord of the manor which we now propose to relate. The manor was, for practical purposes, a kingdom within a kingdom, and the lord made his own rules, which his tenants were compelled to obey. One of these laws was in the direction of establishing a monopoly for his mills. It was enacted that all the cloth made in the town should be fulled at the Abbot's mills, and all the townsmen's corn should be brought to the monastery mills to be ground.

The Albanians set up their own handmills, and refused to send their corn to the Abbot's mills. They likewise declined to recognise the Abbot's right to full their cloth, which they sent to those traders who would do it cheaper. Finding his ordinance evaded, the Lord Abbot sought by forcible means to have it obeyed. Force was met with resistance, and the aggrieved townsmen carried their case to Westminster. " An appeal from the decision of their spiritual lord to a secular judge appeared to the monks no better than sacrilege. They tolled the great bell. They walked in procession singing their penitential Psalms, and invoking the aid of the blessed Alban." Judgment was given in the Abbot's favour on all the points, thus establishing the claims of the lord of the manor. "The townsmen had to surrender their querns, and purchase forgiveness by a present of wine. The Abbot, in turn, promised moderation in the charges which were to be demanded at his mills." Emboldened by their success, the monks made serious encroachments upon the rights of the inhabitants of the manor. They enclosed woods, and preserved fish in streams, to which the people had hitherto had access, besides in various ways seeking to increase the revenues of the Abbey, the extravagance of Abbot Hugh de Eversden having greatly impoverished it. Edward II. had been the friend and patron of Abbot Hugh. In the social and political upheaval which occurred in his later years, the people saw their opportunity. As Madox observes, "They wished rather to be answerable to the king than to an inferior lord, and attempted a stratagem to absolve themselves from their allegiance to the Abbot." They refused to grind their corn at his mills, and set to work to erect their own handmills. They

demanded the restitution of their other privileges,
among them that of returning two members to
Parliament, and attacked the Abbey to enforce
their demands. They were repulsed, and a process
instituted against them. The townsmen petitioned
the monarch, and stated "that they held their
town *in capite*, and were accustomed in the times
of Edward I. and his ancestors to give their
attendance in Parliament by two burgesses, whose
names were enrolled in Chancery, in lieu of
all service, and that nevertheless the sheriff of
the county of Hertford, by the procurement of
the Abbot, had refused to summon the said burgesses," and they prayed the king relief from this
grievance. To this petition reply was made:
"Let the rolls of Chancery be searched, that it
may be ascertained whether the said burgesses
were wont to attend Parliament in the time of our
ancestors or no, and let justice be done as the
necessity of the case requires." A process was
served upon the weak and vacillating Hugh to
restore all the liberties and franchises of the
people of the town upon the same footing as they
were set forth in Domesday. The Abbot yielded
and further consented to the inhabitants choosing
twenty-four of their number to determine the

boundaries of their town, and agreed that all within that area should be burgesses ; also, that the
town should be represented in Parliament as here-
tofore by two burgesses.

The right of free access to the woods was not
conceded, but the people would not be gainsaid.
The late Professor Froude tells the story in
graphic terms. He writes : " The cry rose,
'Give us back our fisheries! Give us back
Barnet Wood! We must have Barnet Wood!'
'The Abbot, hearing these words, and perpending
that the world was at enmity with God's Church
and His ministers,' thought it best to bend
altogether. At once, mad with delight, the boys
dashed off with their nets and lines to the ponds.
The men rushed to the woods, tore down the
fences, and marched back to the town in procession, carrying branches of the trees as a
symbol of their victory." Their successes served
only to increase their insolence, according to
another chronicler, and the townsmen "upon
every occasion exulted with indecent joy at the
victory they had obtained over this timid old
Abbot." Mortified by the concessions which, in
his weakness, he had been compelled to make,
and embittered by his financial embarrassments,

Abbot Hugh died shortly after this dramatic reassertion of the privileges of the burgesses of his demesne.

Abbot Hugh was succeeded by a man of a different calibre. Richard of Wallingford, who was the son of a blacksmith of the town from which his son took his name, ruled the convent with a firm hand. "Abbot Richard was over rigid with us," writes one of his monks. "Partly he was himself to blame, partly his predecessors, who had let us all do as we pleased." His rigid discipline effected a temporary reformation in the habits of the monastic brethren, and his strength of character secured for him a victory over the contumelious townsmen. Abbot Richard bided his time, and it came at last. Though dispossessed of much of his control over the citizens, the Abbot still retained the right to hold courts for the punishment of offenders against morals, which had been granted by a charter to Abbot Henry de Gorham by Henry I., conferring the power "to hold pleas, and take cognisance of all lesser crimes and other offences which had hitherto been punishable by the Leet, the Hundred, or the County Court." The burgesses appear to have refused obedience to him as spiritual lord.

Intoxicated with their success, they disregarded all their moral obligations, and one scandal, more flagrant than the rest, gave the Abbot his opportunity. He resolved, as his chronicler tells us, " *se demonstrare cornutum.*" Professor Froude narrates the story thus, " A citizen of St. Albans, one John Taverner, was living openly with another man's wife. He was a person with whom it was dangerous to meddle, *propter malitiam ipsius Johannis.* The Abbey marshal ventured at last to serve a writ upon him. The mob rose ; Taverner assaulted the marshal ; the marshal defended himself, struck Taverner down, killed him, or, as the chronicler mildly puts it, so wounded him *ut de percussionne idem Johannis postea moriebatur,* that the said John did afterwards die of the blow. The citizens flew to their weapons—swords, lances, pitchforks, sticks, stones, anything that came to hand. Their leaders calmed their fury before they resorted to open violence, and not knowing that times were changed, then indicted the Abbot for the death of their townsman." The result was that the Abbot was acquitted, and, reversing the tables, had the leaders of the riot apprehended and re-examined. He accused the burghers of having extorted their charters from Abbot Hugh by main force and open violence. He succeeded in obtaining "a complete acknowledgement of his power, and the formal surrender of all the privileges which they had wrested from Hugh de Eversden, with all their charters and records."

The circumstances are thus narrated by Walsingham, in his "Chronicles."

"In the sixth year, of Edward the Third, Adam de Usher, John de Neubery and twenty-nine others, townsmen of St. Albans, in Hertfordshire, came into the king's chancery and on behalf of themselves and the rest of the townsmen, and brought their Regal Charter, confirmatory of certain liberties which before that time had been granted to the said townsmen by the writing of Hugh, late Abbot of St. Albans and his convent, and prayed that the said charter might be cancelled and that the enrolment thereof in Chancery might be struck out of the said rolls, and they did there renounce for themselves and their heirs and successors, all the liberties contained in the said charter. At their request the Keeper of the Rolls of the said Chancery broke off the seal of wax from the same charter and cancelled the enrolment thereof made in the Rolls of the said Chancery. Likewise the townsmen brought thither their common seal made of silver, and declared for themselves and their heirs and successors that they ought not to have and would not have any such common seal, and also prayed that the seal might in like manner be destroyed ; and at their request the said seal was destroyed and the silver of it was delivered to Friar Richard de Hedersete, monk of St.

Albans, to be carried to the shrine of St. Alban towards
the charges of the work of that shrine."

Abject as was this submission and surrender
of all their rights—" the disclaimer of all their
Burgensick liberties, and, in a sort, the dissolution
of their corporate body," it was not the depth
of their humiliation. Notwithstanding this disclaimer " in the name and on behalf of themselves
and the rest of their comburgesses," the clever
Abbot had yet more in store. The querns, which
had been the sorest grievance, were seized, and
the millstones carried to the Abbey, and "let
into the pavement of the Abbey ' parlor ' *in
perpetuam rei memoriam.*"

We now come to the last resistance of the
burgesses against the Lord Abbot. Some years
have elapsed since we saw the millstones carried
in triumph to the Abbey cloisters. The year is
1377. The King, Edward, the third of that
name, is dead, and his successor is a mere boy,
Richard II., son of the hero of Cressy and
Poictiers, and grandson of the deceased monarch.
The exactions of the government and the arrogant
assumptions of the nobles, together with the heavy
taxation consequent on the ruinous French wars,
had borne their inevitable fruit. The country was

on the verge of rebellion. The preaching of John
Ball, Froissart's "mad priest," had not been
without effect, and the yeomen of Kent found
other men of the villan class equally ready to rise
in the assertion of their liberty.

The foremost figures in the Peasants' Revolt
were Wat Tyler, John Ball, and Jack Straw.
The men of Hertfordshire were led by one
William Grindcobbe, or Gryncope, as one writer
calls him. Grindcobbe figures prominently on
the stage for some little time, and then, the revolt
being quelled, he disappears tragically. Animated
by aspirations for liberty and a sense of their
degraded condition as serfs, aspirations first
awakened by the teachings of Wycliffe and the
Lollards, the peasants determined to achieve their
liberation. They demanded the abolition of
slavery, declaring that God made all men equal,
and that they had a right to have wages for their
labour, and to live free men ; also, fixed rent,
instead of services, for their holdings, freedom of
trading in the market towns, and the right of
pasturage on common lands, as well for the poor
as for the rich. The rebels had advanced on
London. Jack Straw had made his camp on
Hampstead Heath, where " Jack Straw's Castle "

perpetuates the locality to this day. He afterwards removed to Highbury Barn, and it was
here that the insurgents from Hertfordshire, and
from the town of St. Albans, joined him.   In the
meantime, events had developed in the Abbey
town.   Reinforced by the men of the country-
side, the townsmen menaced the Abbey.   Grindcobbe, a descendant of one of the men who had
wrung the charter from Abbot Hugh, headed the
mob and demanded a restitution of the liberties
from the Abbot, Thomas de la Mere.   The
Abbot proposed a joint conference with the King,
professing himself ready to acquiesce in whatsoever the King commanded.   Intelligence of the
progress of affairs in London had reached St.
Albans, and Grindcobbe, with a chosen body
of armed followers, proceeded thither to confer
with Wat Tyler as to the best means to be
adopted with the Abbot.   He had an old
grievance against the Abbey authorities.   His
house was alleged to encroach upon the Abbey
precincts ; the officers sent by the Abbot to
inspect the premises had been maltreated by
Grindcobbe.   The latter was excommunicated,
and compelled to undergo an undignified penance,
appearing naked before the monks.   It is easy to

imagine his feelings as he proceeded to London. To stay the depredations of the mob the King had acceded to their petitions, and Wat Tyler sent Grindcobbe to the King. Richard granted him an interview, heard the story of the ill-deeds of De La Mere, and gave him a letter to the Abbot to restore the Albanians' privileges, and promised a charter should be sent. The people returned to St. Albans, and again claimed their rights. They threatened dire vengeance "unless licence were given them by the Abbot to hunt in the woods adjoining, and to fish in the waters of the monastery, and unless the Abbot would renounce those rights which had been confirmed to the monastery in the time of Abbot Walling-ford." On entering the Abbey grounds a rabbit started from its hole, was transfixed by a spear, and its body set up in the Market Place as a symbol of free warren. Upon which Walsingham observes :—"Wherefore because they had in-fringed Christ's patrimony their leaders were afterwards dragged over those meadows and through those woods, and then hanged according to their demerits." News was received from the King with a charter for the Abbot to execute, restoring to the townsfolk all the privileges which

Abbot Hugh had conceded. Prevarication was of no avail, Grindcobbe had a thousand men outside the walls, and the Abbot yielded to the demands, voiced by one Richard of Wallingford— one of the chief burgesses, who acted as the King's messenger,—and granted all the men demanded. The danger. was not passed, however. Emboldened by the success of their Albanian compatriots the men of Barnet urged claims in respect to the wood there, which the Abbot was forced to concede. One of the grievances under which the Abbot's tenants laboured were certain tolls and taxes, which, seizing their opportunity, the people of Watford and of Tring determined to be rid of. They crowded into the Abbey, and demanded the remission of these hated imposts. The Abbot was not in a position to refuse. One dramatic act yet remained to be performed. Jubilant at their manumission, the mob forced their way to the " parlor," from the floor of which they tore up the mill-stones, which the triumphant monks had placed there as a token for all time of the townsmen's submission. It was now the hour of the monks' humiliation. The elated burgesses broke up the stones, and distributed the fragments through the town as mementoes of the great event.

The Abbey was now free from further molestation. The burgesses had gained a signal, but, so far as its immediate results were concerned, a short lived triumph. Relying on Richard's frank and generous promise to redress all grievances, and his amnesty for past offences, the mob which had gathered around and in the metropolis quietly dispersed to their homes. Authority once more firmly established the king determined on a great and bloody vengeance. The tragic death of Wat Tyler was but a precursor of a like fate for many of his followers. The King had gone into Essex and Suffolk to suppress the insurrection when news reached him of the doings at St. Albans. He decided to proceed thither immediately to quell the disturbance. Sir William atte Lee, however, volunteered for the service, and entering the town with fifty bowmen he apprehended Grindcobbe and his chief supporters, and threw them into prison, despite "the hostile disposition of the townsmen, and the refractory spirit of the insurgents." Fearing the violence of the people of St. Albans Lee sent Grindcobbe and his chief accomplice to Hertford Gaol. Here they were safely housed and were to have been executed the next day.

The people of the town again rose in revolt,
threatened to sack the Abbey, and fearing lest
they would follow words with actions the monks
despatched messengers to Hertford.   Grindcobbe
was released on bail, promising to surrender a
week later.   He fulfilled his word, and on June
23rd, 1381, he once more surrendered himself to
the authorities at Hertford.   The King and the
Chief Justice Tresilian announced their intention
of coming to Hertford, where it was only too
evident they were determined to execute a like
revenge as in Essex and Kent, where had been
enacted an earlier and scarcely less " Bloody
Assizes," than that which won for Jeffries the
execration of succeeding generations of Englishmen.   Thoroughly terrified for the safety of
Grindcobbe, the Albanians again visited the
Abbot.   They renounced all the privileges and
liberties which they had so recently won, returned
the fragments of the millstones to the "parlor."
They offered gold to the Abbot, but all their
entreaties were powerless to avert the impending
doom.   The Abbot accepted all the signs of
submission, and did not refuse the money, but
he was unable, even assuming he felt so disposed,
to save the riotous Albanians.

Grindcobbe was fetched from Hertford and having been sentenced with thirteen others by Tresilian, they were hanged in the presence of the King. John Ball, whose preaching had instigated the rebellion, had been arrested, and he too was brought to St. Albans where he paid the penalty. He was hanged, drawn and quartered, in the king's presence. Before leaving the town for Berkhamsted, where he proposed to disport himself in the pleasures of the chase, Richard, who was accompanied by an armed force of a thousand men, caused all the men of the town, from the ages of fifteen to sixty, to be brought before him, and there to take the oath of allegiance. The dead bodies of the unfortunate Grindcobbe, the Barber John, and their other associates, had all this while being hanging in chains on the gibbet. During the night following the day that the king left for his hunting expedition at Berkhamsted, the Albanians took down the bodies of their friends and reverently buried them. The news was conveyed to the king, who immediately despatched a peremptory message that the burgesses were to exhume the corpses and re-hang them on the gallows. Thus disastrously ended that memorable assertion of

5

municipal rights, and struggle for liberty from the
control of the Abbot; a sadly dramatic conclusion,
which provoked the spiteful observation of
Walsingham. "Such was the liberty which they
had won for themselves, the liberty of being made
into hangmen."

But the struggle had not been in vain; the
power of the barons was broken, and serfdom
was beginning to disappear, when the Civil
Wars—another epoch of our national history,
some important phases of which were also worked
out in Hertfordshire—finally crippled the lords,
and under the crushing policy of Henry VII.
feudalism vanished entirely. On the suppression of the monasteries, the town reverted to
the Crown as a part of the possessions of the
Dissolved Monastery of St. Albans, and descend-
ing from Henry VIII. to his son Edward VI.,
the latter granted a charter to the burgesses,
confirming them in privileges hitherto enjoyed,
and constituting them "a free Borough, corporate
in deed, fact, and name for ever."

Kings' Palaces.

BY A. WHITFORD ANDERSON, A.R.I.B.A.

"The spider taketh hold with her hands, and is in kings' palaces."
—*Prov. xxx. 28.*

IN a county possessing so many natural advantages as Hertfordshire, and situated so near London, we should naturally expect to find Palaces where Monarchs might lay aside the sceptre for a while, and seek some relief from the cares of a Kingdom. We accordingly find this county to have been a favourite place of residence of our kings from the earliest times. There are many places which have been chosen at one period or another, but I shall confine myself to the three principal ones at Berkhamsted, King's Langley, and Theobalds, on the Essex border.

Berkhamsted Castle.

The town of Berkhamsted lies on the old Roman way of Akeman Street, and from the old coins and other remains found, it has been surmised that a Roman Camp existed here, and there is a curious old tradition that the town

was visited by St. Paul,* who drove away, for
ever, all serpents and thunderstorms. Tradition,
however, fails to explain how the phenomena
returned again to their old haunts, in spite of
the Apostolic prohibition.

Nothing is known of the history of the Castle
before the Conquest, but it seems likely that an
Anglo-Saxon stronghold existed here before that
time, as William met here a deputation of Anglo-
Saxon nobles who came to offer him the crown,
and it was from Berkhamsted that William
proceeded to his coronation at Westminster.

After his coronation William attempted to
march to St. Albans, but was successfully
opposed by Frederick, the last Saxon Abbot,
who caused trees to be felled to block up the
roads, so the Conqueror turned aside to
Berkhamsted, and invited the Abbot to a
friendly meeting. At that meeting the King
took a solemn oath on the relics of St. Alban,
which the Abbot had brought with him for the
purpose, to keep and uphold the ancient Saxon
laws; an oath, which, as is evidenced by his
subsequent conduct, he never had any intention

---

* History of Berkhamsted by J. W. Cobb, to whom I am indebted for
much of the information concerning the Castle.

of keeping. One of the first acts of William
was to confer the manor of Berkhamsted upon
his half-brother the Earl of Moreton, who seems
to have strengthened the Castle considerably
and occupied it himself. We have no record of
the Conqueror having stayed here again, nor of
his successor William Rufus having done so, but
Matthew Paris relates a curious story concerning
the death of the last named monarch, in which
Moreton, or his son, figures. It is said that the
Earl, when hunting one day in the New Forest,
was met by a black goat, bearing the body of
Rufus, black, naked, pierced through the heart,
and covered with blood. Moreton adjured the
goat by the Holy Trinity to tell him what he
carried, and the goat replied, "I am carrying
your King to judgment; yea, that tyrant William
Rufus, for I am an evil spirit, and the revenger
of the malice which he bore to the Church of
God; it was I who caused this his slaughter;
for the Proto-martyr of England (St. Alban)
commanded me to do so, who complained to
God of him for his grievous oppressions in this
Isle of Britain, which he first hallowed."

In 1104, Moreton's son Henry, having rebelled
in Normandy against Henry I., was imprisoned,

his eyes were put out, and his estates were
forfeited, and Berkhamsted was bestowed by the
King upon his arrogant favourite and Chancellor,
Randulph, who rebuilt the Castle, and invited
Henry to visit him, and see the work he had
done. The King, therefore, proceeded to Berkhamsted, and there witnessed what the old
chronicler, Henry of Huntingdon, calls "a
manifestation of God, worthy of Himself," for
as Randulph was boastingly showing his Castle
to the King, he fell from his horse, and was so
hurt that he died in a few days.

The next we hear of Berkhamsted is during
the reign of Henry II. who granted the manor to
no less a person than Thomas à Becket, who
appears to have lived here in great state, and
after his death, Henry, on several occasions,
held his Court here, and in 1156 he granted the
town its first Charter. During John's reign the
Castle was granted to the good Geoffrey Fitz-
Piers, Earl of Essex, who died in 1212, and his
son Geoffrey de Mandeville espousing the cause
of the Barons against the King, was deprived
of the Castle, which was entrusted to the care
of Richard Fitz-Count, who put it in repair and
held it for the King.

It is a matter of history how the despairing
Barons called in to their aid Prince Louis of
France, and offered him the crown, but we find it
more nearly concerns us, when Louis, who had
captured Hertford, laid siege to Berkhamsted
Castle in the year 1216, and in two weeks forced
the garrison to surrender. According to the old
chroniclers, the Castle was most valiantly
defended, and we are told that, on one occasion,
the besieged made a sudden sally, and surprising
the Barons during dinner, disarmed them and
returned unharmed to the Castle.

After Louis had been finally driven out of the
kingdom, Henry III. bestowed the manor upon
his brother Richard, Earl of Cornwall, afterwards
well-known as the King of the Romans. Richard
repaired the Castle, and, in 1254, he added a new
tower of three stories, much to the discomfort of
the good people of Dunstable, in the adjoining
county of Bedford, who complained of their trade
being injured by reason of their carts being all
impressed to carry timber to Berkhamsted.
Richard's son Edmund succeeded him, and the
Dunstable people seem to have had it out with
him, as we find them stopping, in Dunstable
market, a cart containing fish destined for

Edmund's dinner. Edmund, who founded the neighbouring College of Ashridge, died in 1300, and the manor reverted to King Edward I., who granted it to his second wife Margaret.

Upon her death, Edward II. bestowed the estate upon his favourite, Piers Gaveston, whom we shall again meet with, under less happy circumstances, at the Palace at Langley. It was at Berkhamsted that Gaveston married the King's neice, Margaret de Clare; the King himself was present at the ceremony, which was on a great scale, and he scattered silver pennies, to the amount of £7 10s. 6d., over the heads of the couple on entering the church. After the execution of Gaveston, in 1312, the Castle again reverted to the Crown, and was allowed to fall into disrepair.

It was during the reign of Edward III. that the Castle attained its greatest splendour. He spent a large sum of money in repairing it, and made it one of his chief residences, afterwards granting it to his son, the Black Prince, who spent many years of his life at Berkhamsted, and returned here to end his days after his French victories. He died, however, at Westminster, whither he had gone, in a weak state of health

to meet Parliament. Many were the festive
scenes here during his lifetime, some of which
are chronicled by Froissart, when he was Clerk
of the Chamber to Queen Philippa. Berkhamsted
was also used as a prison for King John of France,
during one of the periods of absence of the Black
Prince.

The next owner, Richard II., did not use it
as a residence, but it was during his reign that
Geoffrey Chaucer acted as Clerk of the Works
here, and at other royal palaces, for a period of
two years. The most glorious days of Berkhamsted were now over, and though some of the
kings continued to take an interest in the town,
it ceased to become a royal residence, though
Henry VI. occasionally visited here, and was
at the Castle when he received news of the
second battle of St. Albans.

Edward IV. granted it to his mother, the
Duchess of York, who resided here until her
death in 1495, the Castle then becoming un-
tenanted fell rapidly into decay. Leland des-
cribing it as "much in ruine" in his time, about
fifty years later. Queen Elizabeth granted the
manor to Sir Edward Cary, of Aldenham, in this
county, grandfather of the "blameless Falkland,"

so celebrated during the Civil Wars ; Sir Edward
demolished the Castle, and employed the material
to build for himself a new house on the hill above,
now known as Berkhamsted House, and where
Charles I. spent a portion of his boyhood,

The old Castle is now a mere mound of earth,
with one or two rough fragments of walling,
though the general plan of keep, wards, moats,
and bastions, can still be traced.

King's Langley Palace.

The Palace of King's, or Chilterne Langley, as
it was known in olden days, to distinguish it from
the adjoining parish of Abbot's Langley, lies on
the main highway between London and Berkhamsted, and formed a convenient resting-place
on the journey. It is not known by whom the
Palace was first erected, but it was probably not
till after the reign of John, or we should surely
have some record of that wandering monarch
having stayed there. The first time we find it
used as a royal palace was in 1294, when Edward
Longshanks spent four months here with his
family and court, to the great dismay of the
inhabitants of the district, who complained that
the King seized all the provisions in the neigh-

bourhood for his own use, and neglected to pay
for them. It seems, however, to have been the
custom of some of our earlier kings, notably King
John,* to travel from one royal manor to another,
so that they might consume the provisions which
were given by their tenants in lieu of rent. In
1299, Edward and his second wife Margaret, to
whom, as we have mentioned, the manor of
Berkhamsted was afterwards granted, again entertained company at the Palace at Langley, and
we trust had, on this occasion, more consideration
for the inhabitants.

Langley was a favourite residence of the
feeble-minded and unfortunate Edward II., who
founded here a Priory and Church of the Friars
Preachers, and built them close to the Palace.
The Church was consecrated in 1312, and the
Priory was at one time said to be the richest in all
England, the Black Friars who had settled there
having evidently found it convenient to dispense
with their vows of poverty. Edward seems to
have resided at Langley in the winter of 1314,
but it is very improbable that there were fes-
tivities on that occasion, as he must have been
mourning the loss of a kingdom, wrested for ever

* Archæologia, xxii., p. 124.

from him by the defeat at Bannockburn, a few months previously.

We have already seen how Edward attended the marriage of his favourite, Piers Gaveston, at Berkhamsted in 1307, but now, in 1315, we find them both at Langley under very different circumstances. The ceremony here is for Edward to lay the remains of his unworthy favourite (who had been executed by the nobles two years before, and whose body had been kept at Oxford), in a tomb in the Priory Church. We read that the King, the Archbishop of Canterbury, and many others, were present, and the funeral was conducted with great pomp, and a monument was raised over his ashes.

On June 5th, 1341, Philippa, wife of Edward III., gave birth to a fifth son at Langley Palace. The child was baptized by Michael de Mentmore, Abbot of St. Albans, and a brilliant tournament was held at Langley in honour of the event. This Prince, afterwards created Duke of York, and who was the founder of the White Rose faction, but was better known as Edmund of Langley, greatly distinguished himself during the French Wars with his brothers, the Black Prince and the Duke of Lancaster. His deeds are chronicled by the poet Harding in a poem which says :—

> "At which Battail Duke John of Gaunt indede
> And his Brother Edmund then fought fell sore.
> Were never twoo better Knightes than thei indede
> That better fought upon a feld afore."

Edmund spent the last few years of his life at
Langley, and, dying in 1402, was, in accordance
with his will, buried by the side of his first wife
Isabel of Castille, in the Priory Church, whence
his remains were removed, along with his tomb,
to the parish church of King's Langley, about
the year 1575, where the tomb may still be seen.
Amongst others who were buried in the Priory
Church were Edward, eldest son of the Black
Prince, who died in 1372, aged seven years, and
Ralph, eldest son of Hugh, Earl of Stafford, who
was assassinated by Sir John Holland at York in
1385, and was buried at Langley with all the
pomp of chivalry.

Langley Palace is associated with the unhappy
King Richard II., who kept Christmas here in
1392, and again in 1396, when he was joined
by his uncle, "old John of Gaunt, time-honoured
Lancaster." It is interesting to note that one of
the scenes in Shakespeare's "Richard II." is laid
in the garden of the Palace at Langley ; it was

there that Richard's queen overheard the gardener
tell of her husband's overthrow, and when she
exclaimed :—

> "Gardener, for telling me this news of woe,
>   Pray God the plants thou graft'st may never grow."

That prayer has been more than amply fulfilled,
as garden, Palace, Priory, and all, are gone, and
only a few stones serve to mark the site. The
spider has surely taken hold with her hands and
entered into this Palace! The saddest scene,
however, yet remains. In 1400, the Priory
Church received the body of the murdered King;
but no pageant marked the funeral rites; we are
told that none of the nobles of the land were
present, and but a small gathering of the common
people, and even the Bishop of Chester, who,
with the Abbots of St. Albans and Waltham, had
performed the last ceremony, were unable to find
any one even to ask them to dinner.

> "Within the hollow crown
>   That rounds the mortal temples of a king,
>   Keeps Death his court; and there the antic sits,
>   Scoffing his state, and grinning at his pomp."

Fourteen years after, Richard's remains were
removed with great pomp to Westminster by
Henry V., who himself resided at Langley during

the first Holy Week after his accession to the throne ; but that was the last of royalty at King's Langley, and after this it fell into decay, and gradually crumbled away.

As I mentioned just now, the tomb of Edmund of Langley, still containing his remains, now stands in the Parish Church. It is an altar tomb, but instead of its original cover, which stands, disused, in the church, part of the old altar slab has been substituted, on which may be seen three out of the original five incised consecration crosses, which were put on in allusion to the five wounds of our Saviour. While in the church, the curious should notice an old printed bill hanging in the vestry, dated January 9th, 1683, referring to the curing of the King's Evil by the touch of Royal hands. It begins :—
" Whereas by the Grace and Blessing of God, the Kings and Queens of this Realm by many ages past have had the happiness, by the Sacred Touch and Invocation of the Name of God, to cure those who are afflicted with the disease called the King's Evil : and his Majesty in no less measure than any of his Royal Predecessors having had great success therein, etc., etc." The words "in no less measure" indicate

commendable caution on the part of His Majesty, King Charles II., a quality that would have stood him in good stead had he applied it to greater Evils than the King's.

The Palace of Theobalds.

The Palace of Theobalds dates from much later times than either of the preceding. In the year 1563, the manor was purchased by the Right Hon. William Cecil, Secretary of State to Queen Elizabeth, and from that date its greatness commences. He built here a magnificent mansion and invited his Royal Mistress to visit him, which she did on no less than fifteen occasions between 1564 and 1598, being splendidly entertained each time. Sir Francis Bacon tells a good story of Elizabeth when residing here. "Queen Elizabeth was entertained by my Lord Burleigh at Theobalds; and at her going away, my lord obtained of the Queen to make seven knights. They were gentlemen of the country, of my lord's friends and neighbours. They were placed in a rank as the Queen should pass by the hall, and, to win antiquity in knighthood, in order, as my lord favoured; though indeed the more principal gentlemen were placed lowest. The Queen was told of it, and said nothing; but when she went along, she passed them all by, as far as the skreen, as if she had forgot it; and when she came to the skreen, she seemed to take herself with the manner, and said, 'I had almost forgot what I promised.' With that she turned back, and knighted the lowest first, and so upward. Whereupon Mr. Stanhope, of the privy-chamber, a while after told her, 'Your Majesty was too fine for my Lord Burleigh.' She answered, 'I have but fulfilled the Scripture, the first shall be last, and the last first.'"

Other writers describe the glories of the mansion in most enthusiastic terms. The Queen raised Cecil to the Peerage under the title of Lord Burleigh. After his death the estate came to his second son, Sir Robert Cecil, afterwards the Earl of Salisbury, who entertained King James I. here for four days, when on his way to take possession of the English throne, and in 1606, James accompanied by the King of Denmark, made another visit to Theobalds, where extravagant amusements, lasting five days, were provided for them. Cussans * quotes the

* History of Hertfordshire.

following amusing incidents, related by eye-witnesses, which occurred on this occasion. At one pageant, in which the King of Denmark represented Solomon, a lady of the court, assuming the character of the Queen of Sheba, and bearing gifts to lay at his feet, had previously imbibed so copiously, that she fell into the lap of the King. His Majesty was graciously pleased to overlook the *contre-temps*, and rising from his throne attempted to dance with the Queen of Sheba. But the royal legs were as unsteady as those of the lady, and King Solomon was ignominiously carried away to his chamber. " Now did appear," writes one of the guests, " Faith, Hope and Charity. Hope did essay to speak, but wine did render her endeavours so feeble that she withdrew. Faith was then all alone, for I am certain she was not joined with Good-works, and left the court in a staggering condition. Charity came to the King's feet; she then returned to Hope and Faith, who were both sick in the lower hall."

James was so delighted with the house and estates of Theobalds, where he could enjoy his love of hunting to the full, that he persuaded the Earl of Salisbury to give him the place in exchange for the Palace of Hatfield, not far distant. The King came into possession in 1608, and enlarged the park, surrounding it with a wall, said to have been ten miles in circumference. After this most of his spare time was spent here, and he died at Theobalds on the 27th March, 1625.

Charles I. was first proclaimed King at Theobalds, and was there in 1642 when Parliament presented the petition before the outbreak of the Civil War, and from this place he set out on March 3rd of the same year to raise his standard at Nottingham.

One would have thought that a magnificent house like Theobalds, built in comparatively recent times, would have survived, but, no! the spider laid hold with her hands there also, and in ten years not a vestige remained, the Palace having been pulled down by order of Parliament, and the materials sold.

After the Restoration, Charles II. bestowed the manor upon General Monk in gratitude for his assistance in restoring the Monarchy, and created him Duke of Albemarle. The title, however, became extinct upon his son Christopher, the second duke, dying without issue in 1688.

Dr. Isaac Watts lived here for thirty-six years, until his death in 1748, at the invitation of his friend and patron, Sir Thomas Abney, who then occupied the estate. The present mansion stands about half a mile south-west of the old Palace.

I think I have written enough to show how intimately Hertfordshire has been associated with the history of our kings, but it seems more than curious that of all the Royal residences,—Berkhamsted, Langley, Theobalds, Hatfield, Royston,—scarcely a vestige remains to remind us of their olden days—one long record of bloodshed and toil and suffering—not unrewarded however, for out of them has been moulded the free and happy England of to-day.

Stately Homes of Hertfordshire.

By Thomas Frost.

"The stately homes of England,
How beautiful they stand !
Amidst their tall ancestral trees,
O'er all the pleasant land."
HEMANS.

Introduction.

THE late Lord Lytton, in opening the meeting of the British Archæological Association at St. Albans in 1869, grouped together the "stately homes" of Hertfordshire in that effective manner which he was so specially qualified for by his long connection with the county, and his intimate knowledge of its historical castles and mansions. "Cashiobury," he said, "was, according to tradition, the royal seat of Cassibelaunus, and passing to the noble family that now held its domains, it found an owner as brave as its old British possessor in the first Lord Capel, faithful in life and in death to the cause of Charles I. King's Langley was the birth-place of Edmund de Langley, the brave son of Edward III., and close beside it was

born Nicholas Brakespeare, afterwards Pope
Adrian IV. Moor Park was identified with the
names of Cardinal Wolsey and the ill-fated Duke
of Monmouth. Sir John Mandeville, the famous
traveller, who, if he invented his travels, certainly
beat them all in the art of romance, was a native
of St. Albans. Panshanger was associated with
the name of Cowper, while the delightful essayist,
Charles Lamb, boasted his descent from Hertfordshire. Future archæologists would revere at
Brocket the residence of the two distinguished
men who swayed the destinies of the country in
our time as first ministers of the Crown, Lords
Melbourne and Palmerston, akin by family
connexion, akin still more by the English
attributes they had in common, an exquisite
geniality of temper, united with a robust and
simple manliness of character. At Hatfield there
still stood the tower from the window of which,
according to tradition, the Princess Elizabeth
envied the lot of the humble milk-maid, and
there was still seen the trunk of the oak under
which she heard the news of her succession to
the throne. And what Englishman—nay, what
stranger from the foreign nations to which,
conjointly with the posterity of his native land,

Francis Bacon entrusted the verdict to be pronounced upon his labours and his name— would not feel that he was on haunted ground when he entered the domains of Gorhambury, and examined the remains of the abode in which the Shakespeare of philosophy united the most various knowledge of mankind with the deepest research into the secrets of nature and the elements of human thought." With this introduction, let us now survey the grand historical mansions which the noble author of "The Last of the Barons" thus passed in review.

Moor Park.

This fine old park is situated between Betchworth Heath and Rickmansworth, in the south-western corner of the county. Being thickly wooded, and the surface very uneven, it presents a wilder appearance than most English parks; but from the same causes the scenery is of a very varied character, the paths meandering through glades and dells, in which the many deer form picturesque groups in the shade of the fine old beeches, some of which are of enormous girth. The domain was originally the property of the abbots of St.

Albans, but became separated from the abbey
lands during the long and sanguinary contest
between the two branches of the Plantagenet
dynasty. Henry VII. granted it to Robert
Vere, Earl of Oxford, who led the van of his
army at the battle of Bosworth; but it again
reverted to the Crown, and in the following
reign was for some time in the possession of
Cardinal Wolsey.

The original mansion, which occupied nearly
the same site as the present one, had a gate-
house, with a tower, admitting into a courtyard,
and was surrounded by a moat. It is said to
have been built by George Neville, Archbishop
of York, in the fifteenth century. It had several
owners afterwards, and about the time of the
Restoration was in the possession of Sir John
Franklyn, whose son sold it to the Earl of
Ossory, son of the Duke of Ormond, by whom
it was again sold, passing into the possession
of the Duke of Monmouth, whose widow sold
it to one Styles, of whom little more than his
name is known.

The mansion was practically rebuilt by the
unfortunate son of the second Charles, but
Styles added to the grandeur of its external

appearance by casing it with Portland stone, erecting a magnificent Corinthian portico, and attaching to it a chapel and offices, connected by Tuscan colonnades. The ceiling of the saloon was painted by Sir James Thornhill, after a picture by Guido, this embellishment alone costing the wealthy owner £3,500. The entire cost of the improvements was more than £150,000, the ball-room figuring for ten thousand of that sum. After the decease of Styles, the mansion and park were purchased by Lord Anson with the united fortunes of two uncles, whose heir he became. The estate had several owners afterwards, one of whom, named Rous, in consequence of a reverse of fortune, demolished the wings in order to make money by the sale of the materials. Styles and his wife had been buried under the chapel, which was in the west wing; and the action of Rous necessitated the removal of their remains, which now lie beneath the lawn adjacent to the west angle of the mansion. The park is about five miles in circumference, and the entire estate comprises nearly four thousand acres, of which Lord Ebury is the present owner.

Cashiobury Park.

Only a few miles from Moor Park, and close
to the little town of Watford, is Cashiobury
Park, the large and handsome mansion of which
is the country residence of the Earl of Essex.
At the date of the Domesday survey, the manor
belonged to the abbey of St. Albans, and so
remained until the dissolution of monasteries,
when it was seized by Henry VIII., who
subsequently conveyed it to Richard Morison,
who was knighted by that monarch, and
employed by him in several diplomatic missions
to Charles V. and other sovereigns of Germany.
Sir Richard was similarly employed by Edward
VI., who also appointed him as one of the
commissioners for the reformation of the
university of Oxford, where he had been
educated. During the reign of Mary he resided
many years abroad, being a staunch Protestant,
and died at Strasburg in 1556.

According to an old writer, Sir Richard
Morison commenced "a fair and large house,
situated upon a dry hill not far from a pleasant
river, in a fair park, and had prepared materials
for the finishing thereof; but before the same

could be half built, he was forced to fly beyond the seas." The building was carried on, however, and completed by his son, and was the home of the family for about one hundred years, when the property passed into the possession of the Capel family, the present owners, by the marriage of Elizabeth Morison, the great grand-daughter of Sir Richard, with Sir Arthur Capel, afterwards created Baron Capel. The son of this couple, also named Arthur, entirely rebuilt the mansion, with the exception of the north-west wing ; and Evelyn, who visited it in 1680, thus describes it in his diary :—"The house is new, a plain fabric, built by my friend, Mr. Hugh May. There are divers fair and good rooms, and excellent carving by Gibbons, especially the chimney-piece of the library. There is in the porch or entrance a painting by Verrio, of 'Apollo and the Liberal Arts.' One room parqueted with yew, which I liked well. Some of the chimney mantels are of Irish marble, brought by my lord from Ireland, when he was lord-lieutenant, and not much inferior to Italian. The lympanum, or gable at the front, is a basso-relievo of Diana hunting, cut in Portland stone handsomely enough. I did not approve

of the middle doors being round, but when the
hall is finished as designed, it being an oval,
with a cupola, it will be a very noble palace.

" The library is large and very nobly furnished,
and all the books are richly bound and gilded ;
but there are no MSS., except the Parliament
rolls and journals, the transcribing and binding
of which cost him, as he assured me, five hundred
pounds. No man has been more industrious
than this noble lord in planting about his seat,
adorned with walks, ponds, and other rural
elegancies ; but the soil is stony, churlish, and
uneven, nor is the water near enough to the
house, though a very swift and clear stream
runs within a flight-shot from it in the valley,
which may be fitly called Coldbrook, it being
indeed excessive cold, yet producing fair trouts.
'Tis pity the house was not situated to more
advantage, but it seems it was built just where
the old one was, which, I believe, he only meant
to repair ; this leads men into irremediable errors,
and saves but a little. The land about is
exceedingly addicted to wood, but the coldness
of the place hinders the growth. Black cherry
trees prosper even to considerable timber, being
some eighty feet long ; they make also very

handsome avenues. There is a pretty oval at
the end of a fair walk, set about with treble
rows of Spanish chesnut trees. The gardens
are very rare, and cannot be otherwise, having
so skilful an artist to govern them as Mr.
Cooke, who is, as to the mechanic part, not
ignorant in mathematics, and pretends to
astrology. There is an excellent collection of
the choicest fruit."

This second Baron Capel was created Earl of
Essex in 1661, and, as mentioned by Evelyn, was
at one time Lord-Lieutenant of Ireland. He
joined the conspiracy against Charles II., however,
and in 1683 was arrested at Cashiobury, on a
charge of being concerned in the Rye House plot,
and committed to the Tower, where he died self-
murdered on the morning the trial of Lord William
Russell commenced. Cashiobury House, as rebuilt by him, remained unaltered until the last
year of the eighteenth century, when the erection
of the present mansion was undertaken by the
fifth Earl of Essex, from the designs of Wyatt.
The general plan is a square, with a courtyard in
the centre. The entrance faces the west, the
apartments occupied by the family being on the
east and south, and the kitchen, servants' offices,

etc., on the north. The entrance is by a porch, eastward of which is the great cloister, with five windows filled with stained glass, and containing the family portraits and other pictures. The saloon branches off from the cloister, between the dining and drawing-rooms. The ceiling is adorned with the painting by Verrio, mentioned by Evelyn as being in the hall of the old mansion.

The dining - room, a fine apartment, with wainscoted walls, is decorated with numerous family and other portraits by Vandyck, Hoppner, and others, in addition to pictures by Wilkie, Landseer, and other modern artists. The drawing-room is a most luxurious apartment, very elegantly and tastefully decorated, containing several handsome cabinets and some very fine examples of the genius of Turner, Callcott, Collins, and other great masters of the modern English school. The library occupies four rooms, and comprises a large collection of rare and valuable books in every branch of literature. In these rooms are still to be seen the fine wood carvings of Gibbons, mentioned by Evelyn as being in the old mansion. Both in these apartments and others are many family portraits by Lely and Reynolds, as well as by the artists already named, besides many good examples of Rembrandt, Teniers, Cuyp, and other masters of the Flemish school. There are also some good specimens of Gobelins tapestry.

The park has an area of seven hundred acres, and is divided by the little river Eade into two parts, termed respectively the Home Park and the Upper Park. Evelyn's description scarcely does it justice, it being well wooded with grand old trees, the growth of centuries, comprising beeches (some of which cover an area of a hundred and fifty feet), Norway firs of gigantic height, oaks, and elms. The gardens are as famous for their horticultural productions as in the time of Evelyn, in this respect rivalling those of Moor Park.

Ibatfielb Ibouse.

This grand old Tudoresque mansion, the grounds of which approach the little town of the same name, is the successor of a more ancient building dating from a period at least as early as the beginning of the twelfth century, when it was one of the many residences of the Bishops of Ely. It was upon several occasions a royal residence, the second son of Edward III. having been born there. The manor became Crown property in the reign of Henry VIII., in the latter part of which the only son of that monarch resided at the old palace until his accession to the throne. His half-sister, Elizabeth, occupied it until she was removed to the Tower on a charge of complicity in the conspiracy and rebellion of Sir Thomas Wyat ; and again from the time when she was permitted to return there, in the guardianship of Sir Thomas Pope, until the death of Mary. There she held her first Privy Council, just before leaving it to ascend the throne. Her successor exchanged Hatfield for Theobalds, near Cheshunt, with Sir Robert Cecil, afterwards Earl of Salisbury, who built the present mansion, which was completed in 1611.

All that remains of the old palace comes into view soon after entering the park by the ancient entrance, which is thought to be of earlier date than the reign of Henry VIII., and a wall several feet thick has been found, which is probably of much earlier date. The apartments occupied by Elizabeth when virtually a State prisoner are in the north part of this old building, which is of dark red brick, partly overgrown with ivy. The banqueting hall is now used as stables and other offices, and has a timber roof springing from grotesque corbel heads. The windows are partly filled with stained glass.

The present mansion is also brick-built, and consists of a centre and two wings, having a portico of nine arches and a lofty tower, bearing the date of 1611. Each wing is surmounted by two turrets, with cupolas. The spacious hall admits to a long passage, open on one side by trellis-work to the lawn. Here is displayed a large collection of ancient and modern arms, ranging from some captured from the Spanish Armada to the spoils of the battle-fields of the Crimea. In the chapel at the end of the north wing is a stained glass window of Flemish work, showing remarkable brilliance of colouring. One of the most magnificent features of this part of the mansion is the grand staircase, at the foot of which is a carved hatch, supposed to be intended to keep the dogs from ascending to the drawing-rooms and bed-chambers. The massive balusters are boldly carved, and a handsome, though some-what gaudy, pendant enriches the ceiling. On the wall are some fine portraits of the Cecils, many of them full lengths, by Lely, Kneller,

7

Vandyck, Zucchero, Reynolds, etc. Near the foot of the stairs is the door of the dining-room, and over it is a white marble bust of Lord Burghley. This apartment is panelled throughout with oak, and has a richly decorated chimney-piece and ceiling. Adjoining are the summer breakfast and drawing-rooms, and the remainder of this wing, on the ground floor, consists of spacious private apartments, furnished in the taste of a bygone time, with massive " fire-dogs " for burning wood. Some of the most valuable pictures are in these rooms, a portion of the collection having been the property of Queen Elizabeth, including many portraits by Zucchero, De Heere, Hilliard, Gerards, and others of the Tudor period. The bed-chambers and dressing-rooms above are furnished in the same heavy and sombre style. The wardrobes are carved in the Jacobean style, and the mantel-pieces of some of the rooms are supported by massive columns, entwined with garlands, or by caryatides and other figures.

The grand staircase also communicates with the upper end of the great hall, which has the noble dimensions of fifty feet by thirty. It is lighted at the upper end by an oriel window, and at the side by three lofty bay-windows. The room is panelled with oak, and the walls are hung with splendid tapestry of Spanish design and workmanship. The ceiling is coved, and divided into ten compartments, filled with the heads of the Cæsars in relief. Above is the spacious apartment known as King James's room, which is lighted by three large oriel windows, or at night by six gilt chandeliers, pendant from an elaborately decorated ceiling, On the walls are full-length portraits of George III. and Queen Charlotte, by Reynolds, and some of the members of the Cecil family. Over the lofty chimney-piece is a marble statue of James I., and on the hearth are massive silver " fire-dogs." The whole of the furniture in this room is richly gilded. From it is entered a long gallery, extending the whole length of the south front to the library, panelled with oak, and having an Ionic screen at each end. The ceiling is elaborately ornamented in gold and colours.

The library has the same grand dimensions as King James's room. Over the chimney-piece is a portrait in Florentine mosaic of Robert Cecil, first Earl of Salisbury. The books, manuscripts, and prints are contained in oak cases, above which

is a series of portraits of royal and noble persons
of the seventeenth and eighteenth centuries.
Among the earlier MSS. are copies of the
chronicles of William of Malmesbury and Roger
Hoveden, and a translation from the French of
" The Pilgrimage of the Soul," once in the
possession of Henry VI.   Those of the Tudor
period include a splendid manuscript on vellum,
embellished with a finely-executed miniature of
Henry VII. ; a treatise on councils by Cranmer ;
Wolsey's instructions to the ambassador sent
to the pope by Henry VIII. ; the depositions
concerning the divorce of Anne of Cleves ; the
forty-two Articles of Edward VI. ; the council
book of Mary ; an emblazoned pedigree of
Elizabeth ; copies of the Duke of Norfolk's
letters concerning Mary of Scotland ; and
numerous documents illustrating the conspiracies
of the Earl of Northumberland, Raleigh, and the
authors of the Gunpowder Plot.   There are also
an extensive series of maps, plans, and charts,
and no less than thirteen thousand letters, extending over the Tudor period and the reign
of James I., and including several autograph
letters of Queen Elizabeth.   Probably no private
library is so rich in State papers and other

historical documents as this of Hatfield House.

A natural panorama of a most interesting character is obtained on a clear day from the windows of the mansion. Westward is seen the venerable abbey church of St. Albans, on the north the extensive woods of Brocket Hall, and eastward Panshanger, the seat of Earl Cowper. Charming views present themselves to the eye from various points in the park, in which are some ancient oaks, including the historical tree beneath which Elizabeth received the messengers who brought to her the news of her accession to the throne, and one which, with a girth of thirty feet, is said to be a thousand years old.

The gardens of this palatial mansion have for nearly three centuries enjoyed a celebrity equal to those of Cashiobury and Moor Park. Both Evelyn and Pepys mention them in their diaries, the latter observing that he had never seen such gardens elsewhere, "nor so good flowers, nor so great gooseberries, as big as nutmegs." The garden on the west side of the house is small, being a square of no more than a hundred and fifty feet, enclosed by a hedge, within which is an avenue of limes surrounding the garden. In the centre of the plot is a rockery, built round a basin, and in each corner a small lawn, with a mulberry tree in each, said to have been planted by James I., and surrounded by flower-borders. The garden facing the east front of the mansion is laid out in the geometrical style of the seventeenth century, and connected with it is a maze. There are two other gardens, on the south front, and the other on the north, to both of which metal gates were placed on the occasion of a visit from the Queen and the Prince Consort in 1846. They were cast in Paris, and both in design and workmanship are very handsome, the coronet and the Cecil crest being finished in gold and colours.

Panshanger House.

Two miles from Hertford, on the west, is Panshanger House, the residence of Earl Cowper, standing in a spacious park, watered by the little river Maran. It cannot be compared, either in antiquity or grandeur, with Hatfield, but it is a large and handsome mansion, surrounded by extensive and tastefully laid out grounds. It was erected at the beginning of the present century by the fourth Earl Cowper, near the site of an older house, dating from the commencement of the last century, and which was then demolished. It presents an imposing appearance from the park, and the principal apartments are large, and fitted and furnished in a handsome and tasteful manner.

"The drawing-room," says Waagen, "is one of those apartments which not only give pleasure by their size and elegance, but also afford the most elevated gratification to the mind by works of art of the noblest kind. This splendid apartment receives light from three skylights, and from large windows at one of the ends; while the paintings of the Italian school are well relieved by the crimson silk hangings. I cannot refrain from praising the refined taste of the English for thus adorning the rooms they daily occupy, by which means they enjoy from their youth upwards the silent and slow, but sure, influences of works of art."

The pictures at Panshanger, especially the fine collection of works of the old masters of the Italian school, are indeed one of the chief attractions of the mansion. There are three or four portraits and figure-paintings of subjects from the Old Testament and Italian legendary lore by Andrea del Sarto. The portrait of that master by himself is described as extremely animated and noble in the conception—"the tender, melancholy, wonderfully attractive, and

finely drawn head very softly executed in a deep,
clear *sfumato* treatment." There is a picture
by Titian, representing three children ; and an
admirably painted Cupid, attributed to Annibale
Caracci, but thought by some connoisseurs to be
from the brush of Domenichino. There are two
fine pictures of the infant Jesus and his mother
by Raffaele, and another by Fra Angelico, which
Waagen· describes as the most beautiful work of
that master with which he was acquainted. There
are also very admirable examples of Guido Reni,
Carlo Dolce, Guercino, Perugino, Correggio,
and Paulo Veronese. Of schools other than
the Italian there are pictures by Vandyck,
Rembrandt, Gaspar Poussin, Teniers, Rubens,
Sir Joshua Reynolds, and Wilson.

Panshanger Park is open to the public, and
well repays a walk through it by tourists or casual
ramblers from Hertford or Hertingfordbury to
Welwyn. In the midst of the beautiful scenery
with which it abounds the river Maran expands
into a lake, in front of the house and the tastefully
laid out gardens. Amongst the many grand old
trees which dot the surface of the park is the
well-known Panshanger Oak, called the Great
Oak as long ago as 1709. The trunk has a

circumference of seventeen feet at the height of five feet from the ground. It is now, however, showing signs of decay.

Knebworth Park.

Rivalling Hatfield in historical interest, and surpassing that grand mansion in the glamour of its associations with the literature of the century now drawing near to its close, is Knebworth, near Stevenage, the ancestral home of the Lyttons. Occupying the highest ground in the county, there was a castle here at or soon after the period of the Norman Conquest, when it was held by Eudo Dapifer. In the reign of Edward I. it was in the possession of a son of that monarch, afterwards passing to the renowned Sir Walter Manny, on his marriage with the eldest daughter of the prince, who, after the death of the historically famous knight—one of the first of those who wore the Garter—continued to hold it with the title of Duchess of Norfolk. The daughter and heiress of that lady conveyed it by marriage to the Earl of Pembroke, but it changed owners again, being afterwards sold to Sir John Hotoft, treasurer of the household to Henry VI. From that family it passed, again by sale, to Sir

Thomas Bourchier, from whom it was afterwards purchased by Sir Robert Lytton, a member of the Privy Council of Henry VII., and also keeper of the wardrobe and under-treasurer to that sovereign. The new owner immediately set about enlarging the building, a work which was carried on by his successor, Sir William Lytton, and completed in the reign of Elizabeth by Sir Rowland Lytton, who held the office of Lord-Lieutenant of both this county and Essex.

Knebworth, as thus enlarged, was a square-built mansion in the early Tudor style of architecture, the east front having been the gate-house of the old castle. It so remained until the early part of the present century, and was for many years only partly inhabited, much of it having fallen into decay. In the meantime, the estate had passed, on the death of Sir William Lytton without issue in 1705, into the possession of the Strode family, in which it remained until Lytton Strode bequeathed it by will to his cousin, William Robinson, on whose death, in 1762, it passed to Richard Warburton Lytton. In 1811, the restoration of the mansion was commenced, when three sides of the old building were de-molished, and the fourth, built by Sir Robert

Lytton, on the model of the old palace at Richmond, in Surrey, was thoroughly restored. The estate had at that time become the property of the Bulwer family, and, in 1843, was given by the will of Mrs. Bulwer, widow of General Bulwer, to her son, Sir Edward Lytton Bulwer, who thereupon assumed the surname of Lytton.

One of the most interesting apartments of this fine old mansion are the banqueting-hall, which still retains the ceiling of the time of Henry VII., the raised music-gallery, the old armour on the walls, and the Elizabethan screen. A door leads from it to the oak panelled drawing-room, where, in the reign of Charles I., the Parliamentary leaders, Hampden, Pym, and Eliot, were wont to meet Sir William Lytton, who was a staunch supporter of their policy and advocate of their principles. The music-gallery communicates with the Round Tower Chamber, whence a corridor leads to a chamber in which Hampden once slept, and which still bears the name of the Hampden Room. Beyond this is Queen Elizabeth's Chamber, in which that redoubtable daughter of her father slept when visiting Knebworth, which she did on several occasions. In the library, which is fitted in the Tudor style,

there are a pair of bronze candelabra, inlaid with
silver, which were dug up in Apulia, on the site
of the palace of Joanna, Queen of Naples, and
supposed to be genuine Roman antiquities.

A double flight of stairs, with carved balus-
trades, walls adorned with family portraits, old
armour, and trophies of arms, and windows
emblazoned with armorial bearings, leads to the
State apartments, the first of which has carved
panels, leather hangings, embossed and gilded,
and an armorial ceiling. A long ante-room, hung
with tapestry, communicates with an oval drawing-
room, and thence with the great drawing-room,
which was the presence-chamber of Tudor times,
and has an armorial ceiling and windows emblazoned with armorial bearings, containing nearly
a hundred quarterings. In this apartment are
some portraits of considerable historical interest,
many good examples of the Italian and Dutch
schools of art, specimens of armour from the
time of the Crusades to the civil war of the
seventeenth century, and some rare old furniture
of the period of the first and second Tudors.

The principal entrance to the park from the
main road is by an ivy-covered gate-house,
formerly the east front of the mansion. When

Mrs. Bulwer undertook her work of restoration,
it was taken down, and, the stones being carefully
numbered, was re-erected in its present position
without any alteration, an example that was
followed when Temple Bar was taken down,
and removed to its new location at Theobalds.
The wooded slopes and fine avenues of trees
give a charming aspect to the park, which, in
the opinion of some persons, is not improved by
the obelisks, busts, and artificial ruins placed by
the late Lord Lytton in the neighbourhood of the
lake, or by the mausoleum erected by him in a
sequestered dell.   This was evidently not the
opinion of the noble owner, who, in one of a
collection of essays, etc., published in 1835, gives
a charming description of the park and its
immediate surroundings.

   "The place," he says, "has something of the
character of Penshurst, and its venerable avenues,
which slope from the house down to the declivity
of the park, giving wide views of the opposite
hills, crowded with cottages and spires, impart to
the scene that peculiarly English, half stately and
wholly cultivated, character which the poets of
Elizabeth's day so much loved to linger upon.
As is often the case with similar residences, the

church stands in the park, at a bow-shot from the
house, and formerly the walls of the outer court
nearly reached the green sanctuary that surrounds
the sacred edifice. The church itself, dedicated
anciently to St. Mary, is worn and grey, in the
simplest architecture of ecclesiastical Gothic, and,
standing on the brow of the hill, its single tower,
at a distance, blends with the turrets of the house,
so that the two seem one pile. Beyond, to the
right, half-way down the hill, and neighboured by
a dell girded with trees, is an octagon building
of the beautiful Grecian form, erected by the
present owner ; it is the mausoleum of the family.
Fenced from the deer is a small surrounding
place, planted with flowers—those fairest children
of the earth, which the custom of all ages has
dedicated to the dead. The modernness of this
building, which contrasts with those in its vicinity,
seems to me, from that contrast, to make its
objects more impressive. It stands out alone in
the venerable landscape, with its immemorial
hills and trees—the prototype of the thought of
death — a thing that, dealing with the living
generation, admonishes them of their recent lease
and its approaching end. For, with all our
boasted antiquity of race, we ourselves are the

ephemera of the soil, and bear our truest relation,
so far as our mortality is concerned, with that
which is least old."

"The most regular and majestic of the avenues
I have described," continues Lord Lytton,
"conducts to a sheet of water that lies towards
the extremity of the park. It is but small in
proportion to the domain, but is clear and deep,
and, fed by some subterranean stream, its tide is
fresh and strong beyond its dimensions. On the
opposite bank is a small fishing cottage, whitely
peeping from a thick and gloomy copse of firs and
larch and oak, through which shine, here and
there, the red berries of the mountain ash; and
beyond this, on the other side of the brown moss-
grown deer paling, is a wood of considerable
extent. This, the further bank of the water, is
my favourite spot. Here, when a boy, I used to
while away whole holidays, basking indolently in
the noon of summer, and building castles in that
cloudless air until the setting of the sun. The
reeds then grew up, long and darkly green, along
the margin; and though they have since yielded
to the innovating scythe, and I hear the wind no
longer sigh amidst those earliest tubes of music,
yet the whole sod is still fragrant, from spring to

autumn, with innumerable heaths and wild-flowers, and the odour of the sweet thyme."

Hertford Castle.

Of the old castles of Hertfordshire, only those of Hertford and Berkhampsted (now called Berkhamsted Place, which is dealt with by another hand,) are inhabited at the present day. Hertford Castle was erected by Edward the Elder, at the beginning of the tenth century; but it made no figure in history until the reign of John, when it stood a siege by the revolted barons and their French allies, and, after a stout defence, fell into their hands. It reverted to the Crown, however, and in 1357 was the residence of Queen Isabella, the wife of Edward II. In the book of her household expenses, we read of a journey from Tottenham to Hertford, and the presentation of gifts by the royal lady to the nuns who met her at Waltham Cross. These accounts dispose of the statements made by most historians of her having died at Castle Rising; for they mention numerous journeys of medical attendants and bearers of messages during the month she laid ill at Hertford, where her corpse rested in the chapel of the Castle until removed to London. Here, too, in 1362, died the wife of David II., King of Scotland, and sister of Edward III., during whose reign both the Scottish monarch and John, King of France, were held here in captivity for some time as prisoners of war. In 1369, the Duke of Lancaster, afterwards Henry IV., held a court here at which the deposition of Richard II. was pronounced. The original fortress is no longer in existence, though portions of the old wall and the foundations of one of the towers still remain. The building which long ago took its place passed from the Crown to the Cecils, and in comparatively recent times it was used as a preparatory school for Hailey-bury College. It is now a private residence, one of the wings having been removed, and the whole building reduced in size.

Bishops' Stortford Castle.

This castle can no longer be counted among the "stately homes" of the county, for only the ruins now exist, and very little of them; but in the Norman and early Angevin reigns it was one of the country residences of the Bishops of London. In the reign of Stephen it was

considered a fortress of so much consequence
that the Empress Maud endeavoured to obtain
possession of it in exchange for other property,
but could not prevail upon the bishop to part
with it. It was partially demolished by John,
in revenge for the part taken against him by
the bishop in his quarrel with the Pope. The
portion left standing was used in later times as
a prison, but was demolished in 1640, with the
bridge over the Stort leading to it. Some
remains of the walls, which are of great thickness,
are still to be seen in the cellars of a public-house,
which now occupies the site. "To such base
uses may we come, Horatio."

Sopwell Nunnery.

When this once famous establishment was
secularised, at the time when all the monastic
institutions in the country were suppressed by
Henry VIII., it was granted to Sir Richard
Lee, who, according to Newcome, was indebted
for the favour to the solicitations of his wife,
who had won the regards of the amorous
monarch. Sir Richard enlarged and altered the
building to adapt it for a private residence, and
converted the surrounding grounds into a park,

enclosing them with a wall. He died in 1575, when the estate passed into the possession of Sir Edward Sadlier, who had married his eldest daughter. About the time of the restoration of monarchy, in the seventeenth century, the heiress of the Sadliers conveyed it by marriage to Thomas Saunders, of Beechwood, who afterwards sold it to Sir Harbottle Grimstone, of Gorhambury. The mansion is now in ruins. The nunnery, the site of which they occupy, was of the Benedictine order, and was founded, about the middle of the twelfth century, by Geoffrey de Gorman, abbot of St. Albans. Grants of land were afterwards given to the establishment by Henry de Albini and other members of that family, and also by Richard de Tany.

An Ancient Grammar School.

By A. E. GIBBS, F.L.S.

A PROMINENT place among the historical institutions of Hertfordshire must be given to the ancient Grammar School at St. Albans. If the renown of an educational establishment depended on age alone, there is probably no school in England which would surpass this one. Long before Eton, Harrow, or Rugby was thought of, St. Albans Grammar School was flourishing ; it had even attained a respectable old age before William of Wykeham founded his great school at Winchester. The actual date of its establishment is lost in the dim mists of antiquity. Some assign its foundation to Ulsinus, the Saxon Abbot, who ruled the great monastery of St. Albans in the middle of the tenth century, and who, we know, built the three parish churches at the three principal entrances to the town, dedicating one to St. Michael, the first among the angels, the second to St. Stephen, the first martyr for the faith, and the third to St. Peter, the first of the Apostles. Ulsinus was a man of action, and devoted his energies to building a town round the monastery and encouraging people from the country districts to settle in it, so it is not impossible he may have been the father of the Grammar School.   There is, however, no direct evidence, and the statement must be treated as a mere speculation, and taken for what it may be worth.   But though we do not know when and by whom the school was first established, there is documentary evidence in existence which shows that at the end of the eleventh or early in the twelfth century a large and flourishing school was being carried on under the patronage and control of the Abbots.   The monastic records state that during the rule of Richard de Albini (1097-1119), the school was of sufficient importance to warrant that Abbot sending to Maine to bring over a very clever man named Geoffrey de Gorham to take charge of it.   The journey in those days was a tedious one, and the new master was so long in coming that the Abbot could not wait, and when Geoffrey arrived in St. Albans he found that the vacancy had been filled.   He therefore retired into the Priory at Dunstable, where he supported himself by giving lectures, and waited for the next vacancy.   While there he wrote a sacred play called " St. Catherine," and, in order to perform it, borrowed a number of vestments from St. Albans.   Misfortune appears to have followed poor Geoffrey, for his house caught fire, and the borrowed garments, together with his precious library of books, were totally consumed.   Not knowing in what way he should restore the loss to God and his church, he decided to give himself up as a whole burnt sacrifice, and assumed the religious habit in the monastery of St. Albans, where in the course of time he was elected to the Abbacy.   This early reference to the performance of a Miracle Play is exceptionally interesting.

The next mention we get of the school is in 1195, when we read of the death of the then Master, Alexander Nequam, "a learned doctor," and the appointment of his successor, who was Warren, nephew of the Abbot of the same name. The old chronicler tells us that at this period the school "had the greatest number of scholars of any in England," and that it "was in such repute that it was scarcely surpassed by any other in the kingdom at that time, either in the number of scholars or the utility of the sciences taught." Warren belonged to a learned family ; he and his

two uncles, Abbot Warren and Matthew, being
commonly alluded to as " the threefold cord which
could not be broken."

As we sail down the stream of time we now
and again get glimpses of our school ; a bequest
is left to it, or a charter granted, but, as might be
expected, it is no easy matter to trace its history
in these early days.   Lengthy periods elapse
without any record of its existence appearing, but
it was doubtless doing a good work and flourishing
under the care of the abbots, who forbade anyone
living under the jurisdiction of the Monastery
to attend any other school.

The turbulence and unrest of the Middle Ages
is reflected in a set of rules which were drawn up
for the good of the school.   Rows between town
and gown were frequent ; burgesses and monks
were often at loggerheads, and the young bloods
of the school no doubt enjoyed a good square
fight with the street lads.   So it was found
necessary to forbid the students to carry arms, or
to wander about the streets and roads without
reasonable cause.   Nor were they allowed to
quarrel among themselves or to strike a master.
If a scholar inflicted a light blow upon a fellow
student, or displayed ill-temper, his hood was to

be taken from him by the porter, and the vice-monitor was to punish him ; more serious assaults were dealt with by the master himself. A porter was to sit at the door and prevent scholars from going out two or three at a time and in company. In school the ushers or bachelors were not to display ill-temper or make a noise, while any persons daring to lay rash hands on the masters, or attempting any mischief against them, were to be excommunicated and to receive salutary discipline in the school from all the bachelors. These interesting rules give us an idea of the government of the school in the early years of the fourteenth century. From them we gather that it was the master's duty to enforce discipline, to conduct the examinations, and to distribute the dole to the indigent scholars who received a free education. He was assisted by the bachelors or ushers, who were all to be university men, and were liable to be dismissed by the master. There were two classes of scholars—poor scholars and ordinary scholars. The former, sixteen in number, were boarded in the almonry, and received a free education for five years. They had to wear a choristers' tonsure, and cut their hair in clerks' fashion, and it was part of their duty to say daily

the "Matins of Our Lady" for themselves, and
on festivals "The Seven Psalms" for the convent
and founders.   The ordinary scholars paid fees in
the usual way, and studied Latin grammar and
prose and verse from the large volume which
the school possessed, and which the master had
to take an oath to protect well.

For something like two hundred years we lose
sight of our school, until, in 1480, we light on
"One sometyme scholemayster of Saynt Alban,"
who had set up a printing press and used types in
the town.   What his name was we do not know,
but it is certain that he issued eight works, two of
which were in English, and the rest in Latin.
We may fairly assume that this early printer, who
was carrying on his work at St. Albans while
Caxton was labouring at Westminster, was at one
time the Master of our St. Albans school.   That
he kept a school in the town we know for certain,
and if the educational monopoly conferred by
charter in 1310 was still enjoyed, and there is no
reason to suppose the contrary, it follows that this
ancient establishment can boast of once having
been under the government of a man who holds
almost as honoured a place in the roll of English
typographers as Caxton himself.   How much

interest centres round this unknown schoolmaster-printer! Did he set up his press in the schoolhouse on Hokerhulle, now called Rome Land (*i.e.*, the roomy or waste land), near the west front of the great monastic church, or did he, as seems probable, relinquish his scholastic position to handle the strange-looking wooden types? Did he cut his own letters? if not, whence came they? These, and many other problems present themselves to our minds in thinking about this pioneer of the printing press. Soon after this time there was established at Stevenage, a small town a few miles distant, a new factory for paper, for which we are told there was a great demand, consequent upon the introduction of the art of printing.

But a day of doom was at hand for the monasteries, and when the Abbey of St. Albans fell the Grammar School was buried in its ruins. The ancient schoolhouse was probably sold or bestowed upon a royal favourite when the possessions of the convent were scattered. For a while the time-honoured seat of learning ceased to exist. Richard Boreman, of Stevenage, was the last of a long line of mitred abbots who for centuries had held almost absolute sway over a large track of country, and when he had surrendered

up his abbey to the Commissioners and retired
into a life of greater privacy, it appears that he did
not entirely lose his interest in St. Albans and its
school, for there has lately been brought to light
among the additional Chantry Certificates at the
Public Record Office,* one returned in 1548 in
which there is a note against the return for the
Guild or Fraternity of the Charnel House in St.
Peter's Churchyard, St. Albans, that "Rich. Bawr-
man, late abbote of Seynt Albons, sueth to
purchase this and to erect a scole there."   How
far the old monastic school had been available for
the instruction of the youth of St. Albans we do
not know, but this note appears to show that
when it ceased to exist, the want of a school in
the town was felt, and that Boreman was anxious
to provide one.

When we reach the year 1553, we find ourselves
standing on firmer ground.   The pre-Reformation
history of the school is of necessity enshrowded
in a good deal of obscurity.   Documentary
references to it are few and far between, but as
we have seen there is sufficient evidence in
existence to prove that it was an institution of

* See Note by Mr. William Page, F.S.A., in "Middlesex and Herts.
Notes and Queries," III., 208.

importance in the reign of the first Henry, if not
in that of his brother the Red King, and that it
may even have been flourishing in Saxon times.
When the dissolution of the monasteries came it
fell upon evil times and was suppressed.   It is pro-
verbially darkest before dawn, and so it proved
in the case of the St. Albans Grammar School,
for a successor arose to the old monastic establishment in which was worthily carried on the
educational work for which the town had been so
long famous.

In the last year of the reign of the boy King,
Edward VI., a charter of privileges was granted
to the burgesses of St. Albans, which among
other things provided for the establishment of a
school, as one of the Free Schools which are
associated with the name of that monarch.   The
church had been purchased by the burgesses for
parochial purposes, and it contained a great deal
more room than was needed for public worship.
The beautiful eastern chapels were therefore
appropriated as a school house, and a public path
was cut right through the sacred edifice, by which
the school was separated from the other parts of
the building.   Until a few years ago this passage
divided the grand old church into two parts,

but fortunately this state of things no longer exists. In its new home the school was carried on until quite modern times, and it is easy to imagine the havoc wrought by successive generations of mischievous schoolboys.

These chapels, at one time magnificent specimens of fourteenth century work, fell into a state of ruin. The rich decorated tracery of the windows was ruthlessly destroyed, and wherever a delicate piece of carving offered an opportunity for mischief, the schoolboy's pocket-knife or hockey stick was only too readily wielded. Fortunately these beautiful chapels have now been restored to something like their original condition.

But to return to the sixteenth century. During the reign of Queen Elizabeth, there resided at Gorhambury, near St. Albans, a man of great influence at Court, who was no other than Sir Nicholas Bacon, father of Francis Bacon, the great philosopher. The original charter had given the Mayor and Burgesses of St. Albans power to receive endowments for the maintenance of the school to the extent of £40 per annum, but it is probable that money did not come in so readily as was anticipated. It therefore became necessary to find some other way of providing funds, and a rather novel expedient was hit upon. Sir Nicholas Bacon, the Lord Keeper, was a good and powerful friend of the school, and he used his influence with the Queen to obtain a Wine Charter for the town. Under the provisions of this curious document, the Mayor and Burgesses were empowered to grant two licences for the sale of wine in St. Albans and neighbourhood, and the money which was paid for them was to go to the support of the school. By a later charter the number of licences was raised to three. This privilege still exists; St. Albans, Oxford, and Cambridge being the only towns in England which have the right of issuing their own licences independently of the Excise authorities.

Sir Nicholas took a close interest in the school and all that concerned it. No doubt it was he who induced Master John Thomas, better known as Hilocomius, from the place of his birth, to come over from Bois-le-Duc in Holland to take charge of the school. It is a curious fact that both the first master of the school of whom any record is known to exist, Geoffrey de Gorham, and the first post-Reformation master whose name is preserved should have been foreigners. But no doubt Sir Nicholas Bacon chose his man carefully and well.

John Thomas was both learned and pious; a capable teacher, and a good Christian. A letter from him, addressed to the rector, is still preserved among the St. Albans Corporation papers, and in it he pleads on behalf of a poor townsman who had fallen on evil days. Goldsmith's schoolmaster was "passing rich on forty pounds a year"; John Thomas was content with twenty, and his usher with ten; though taking the comparative value of money then and now these were not inadequate stipends. It is probable that in him the Lord Keeper, who was himself a studious man, found a congenial spirit. Under John Thomas the school appears to have flourished, the students in 1587 numbering "three score and fourteen." He was buried in the Abbey church, and a mural tablet to his memory bears an inscription by John Westerman, who was probably a kinsman of his, and who was himself, in 1625, appointed master of the school. The will of John Thomas Hilocomius is still in existence, and is an interesting document.* It bears date 18th Nov., 38 Eliz. (1595), and commences in the way with which all searchers of old wills are so familiar : " In the name of God. Amen. I, John Thomas Hilocomius,

* A copy of it will be found in " The Herts. Genealogist," vol. II, p. 316.

Scholem^r of the Towne of St. Albanes, in the Countie of Hartff, being sicke and weake in bodie, but of perfecte mynde and memorie (praised be God), doe make and ordeyne this my last will and testamente in manner and forme followinge, that is to saie, ffirste I comende my soule into the handes of Almightie God, and my bodye to be buryed w^thin the Parrishe Churche of St. Alban in such comelie and decent place of the same churche as by my welbeloved wiefe shal be thought meete and convenient." He then proceeds to dispose of his property, bequeathing £3 to the poor of St. Albans to be distributed on the day of his burial; £10 to the ministers and elders of the Dutch Church in London for the benefit of the poor people connected therewith; and £10 to the Mayor and Burgesses of St. Albans to be for ever employed for the continual "settinge on worke" of the poor of the town. In connection with this latter bequest he makes a curious stipulation, which could not have been very flattering to the civic fathers. He says that inasmuch as previous gifts have been by the negligent and evil employment of the said Mayor and Burgesses consumed and utterly wasted, he directs that the authorities shall enter into a bond of fifteen pounds to devote

this legacy to its proper uses.   Whether this bond
was executed is not known, but it is very certain
that the charity has long ago disappeared.   His
books he gives to his friend, William Westerman.
" Rest to the souls of these fine old pedagogues
who during their lifetime taught the youth of St.
Albans to read Greek and Latin, and saw that
they obeyed the rules of the school, and at their
death left of their savings to supply the bodily
wants of their less fortunate neighbours.

The rules drawn up by Sir Nicholas Bacon for
the government of the school are preserved, and
from them we get an idea of the life led by a
schoolboy three hundred years ago.   Daily
attendance at Divine Service is enjoined, and
due provision is made for the religious education
of the boys.   School hours commenced at six in
the morning in summer and seven in winter, and,
with the exception of an interval from eleven till
one, lasted until five o'clock.   On Saturdays and
half-holidays the boys were allowed to go home
at three in the afternoon, but if a scholar were
absent more than three days a quarter he was to
be expelled.   The number of boys was limited to
120, and poor men's children were to have the
preference, but none were to be admitted unless

9

they knew "their accidence without book" and could "write indifferently." Parents were to provide their boys with material for their work, the list of articles required embracing ink, paper, pens, wax candles for winter, a bow, three arrows, bowstrings, a shooting glove, and a bracer to exercise shooting. It is evident from this that in providing for the mental and religious welfare of the boys their bodily training was not over-looked. Archery and other manly sports were encouraged, the boys being fitted to discharge their duties and maintain their rights as free-born Englishmen.

There is in the possession of the governors of the school an old account-book, dating from the year 1587, in which there are numerous entries of great interest. Among other things we find charges for mending windows "broken by rude boys," and also sums collected from the parents of those scholars who had been guilty of the same offence. We get occasional mention of the "yron cradle to make fyre in for the schollers," and of a new frame for them to stand about the hearth when they use the fire in winter. Can we not in imagination picture these schoolboys of three hundred years ago arriving at the school at seven o'clock on a cold, dark winter morning, many of

them having had to walk to the town from remote
country hamlets ?   We see them crowding round
the railing which enclosed the charcoal fire in the
"yron cradle," to supply fuel for which each boy
contributed his quota, and then commencing their
work by the light of the wax candles, placed in
the ten candlesticks which had cost the governors
£2 13s., besides sundry small sums for bringing
them from London and setting them up.

In the seventeenth century, as we find from
these accounts, there gradually grew up a custom
of expending sums of money upon feasting and
enjoyment whenever an opportunity for doing so
occurred.   The governors and schoolmaster used
to meet together and dine or spend a convivial
evening at the expense of the charity, and on one
occasion as much as £2 15s. od. is entered as
having been laid out in this way.   Breaking-up
time, too, was marked by jollity and indulgence.
In the accounts for 1676-7 the item appears :—
"Spent upon the schoolmaster and visitors and
the company when the scholars brooke up 3
several times, £3 11s. od."   Some idea of the
programme carried out on these occasions may be
gleaned from the following entries which were
made a few years earlier :—

Itm, payd the drummer for drumming when the
    boys broke up the 15th October, 1662   2s.

Itm, payd the Musicke for playing the severall
    sounds when the boys acted the two
    comodies of Lingua and the Jealous Lovers
    at two of their breakings up - - - 10s.

Itm, given to the boys that acted - - - 5s.

This sort of thing, however, did not commend itself to the Mayor and Aldermen, for when the governors rendered their accounts in 1677 a resolution was passed ordering that the sum expended upon the schoolmaster, visitors, and the company at the several breakings up should not exceed twenty shillings.

From the sixteenth century to the present day King Edward VI.'s Grammar School has carried on its beneficent work. Generation after generation of English boys have here been given an education which has made them fit to fight the battle of life, among them being many distinguished men, of whom we speak with pride, and whose names are written in their country's roll of honour. At times the fortunes of the school have fallen to so low an ebb that the boys have scarcely numbered a dozen all told. There are Albanians still living who remember the days when the master regarded his post as a sinecure, considering his duty to be discharged when he had drawn his salary. Fortunately those days are gone for ever.   Thirty years ago the school was removed from the Lady Chapel of the church in which it had been carried on for so long a time.   The Great Gate-house of the monastery, until then used as a prison, was found to be available, and, as it offered the necessary accommodation, was purchased.   A picturesque old pile is this ivy-covered Gate-house, standing under the shadow of the Abbey Church, now the Cathedral of the diocese, and surrounded by the green fields which were once covered by monastic buildings.   Excepting the church itself it is the only part of the monastery still standing, and it therefore affords a fitting home for an institution which is the direct successor of the school which first came into being through the instrumentality of the abbot and convent.   New buildings are added when occasion requires, to provide the necessary accommodation for the large and increasing number of boys who apply for admission.

As the past history of the school has been a glorious and honourable one, so its future prospects are bright and promising.   May the St. Albans Grammar School long flourish in its new, yet venerable home!

Waltham Cross.

By the Rev. J. H. Stamp, a.k.c.

THE ancient Memorial Cross, which has given its name to the locality in which it stands, is one of the original monuments erected by King Edward I., to perpetuate the memory of his beloved consort, Eleanor of Castile. It is situated in the urban district of Cheshunt, about twelve miles north of London, at the extreme south-east of Hertfordshire, and near the borders of Essex and Middlesex. *Waltham Cross* was made a separate ecclesiastical parish during the present century, and is not to be identified with the neighbouring parish of Waltham Holy Cross or Waltham Abbey, which is situated in Essex, and derives its name of Holy *Cross*, not from the Eleanor Memorial, but from the grand old Norman church, built in honour of the symbol of the Christian faith by King Harold II., who found within its sacred walls a last resting-place.*

Queen Eleanor has always been regarded as a model of conjugal affection. She was the faithful

* Fuller's History of Waltham Abbey.

and constant companion of her husband, both in pleasure and peril. Before his accession to the throne of England, she had accompanied him on his crusade to the Holy Land, and, when urged by her friends not to hazard her life in this way, she quietly observed that the way to heaven was as near from Palestine as from England, and that nothing should part asunder those whom God had joined together. The tradition, which asserts that she saved her husband's life at Acre, at the risk of her own, by sucking the poison from a wound caused by the dagger of the assassin, appears to be a mere legend. It needs no story of this description to prove her wonderful devotion to him, for her presence in that perilous expedition shows her readiness to sacrifice her life for his dear sake. Nor did her affection for her royal consort ever diminish, for, eighteen years after his accession, she accompanied him on his march to Scotland. On arriving at Herdeby, or Harby, in the parish of North Clifton-upon-Trent, five miles from Lincoln, she was taken ill with a slow fever, and notwithstanding the unremitting attention of physicians and nurses, and the earnest prayers of her sorrowful husband, she succumbed to the foul disease on the 27th or 28th of November, 1290.

Her lifeless body was immediately removed to Lincoln, and there embalmed. The King having determined that the remains should be interred with all due honour at Westminster, the funeral cortege set out from Lincoln Cathedral on December 4th, and, instead of taking the direct road to London, it traversed by a circuitous route, so that it might pass through a more frequented part of the country, where the Queen was well known and beloved, and where it might find a suitable resting-place, at every stage of the journey, in a great church or religious house, so that the faithful might assemble there in large numbers to pray for the repose of her soul. The King took his place in the procession as chief mourner, and the funeral train, as it proceeded on its melancholy way, must have presented one of the most solemn and impressive spectacles that England has ever witnessed. It was received with tokens of the highest respect and deepest reverence at every halting-place, both by clergy and people. Solemn requiems were sung all night by the priests and monks, where the body rested, and on the morrow, shortly after its departure, a suitable site was chosen and consecrated for the erection of a Memorial Cross.

Crosses, as memorials of the faithful departed, had been set up from the early days of Christianity, not only on or near their graves, as at the present time, but also by the wayside, to perpetuate their memory, to secure the prayers of the faithful on their behalf, and to remind all who passed by, that they too must die, and should prepare for that dread event by looking to Him who was crucified for them. But the erection at the place where the funeral procession halted, on its way to the sepulchre, was of very rare occurrence. The idea was probably suggested to the mind of King Edward, by the crosses which had been set up in France, to the memory of his kinsman, King Louis the Ninth, the Saint Louis of the French Monarchy, who had accompanied him when he and his lamented consort set out on their crusade, twenty years before the death of Eleanor. Louis died at Tunis, and his body was brought to Paris, and carried on men's shoulders to St. Denys, where it was interred. After the funeral, memorial crosses were erected, wherever the bearers had rested, to mark the halting-places of the solemn procession, on the road from Mount Cenis to St. Denys. King Edward therefore adopted that which appears to be the only precedent in history. It would naturally commend itself to him as worthy of imitation, on account of its association with his royal and saintly kinsman, who, like himself and his beloved Queen, was a descendant of his predecessor on the throne of England, King Henry II.*

Now, in his pious intention to set up these unique memorials of conjugal love, the King was actuated by a two-fold motive. He desired, in the first place, that her name should be kept in everlasting remembrance in the kingdom, which she had adorned for so many years as one of its brightest ornaments. But above all, in his loving solicitude for her eternal welfare, he was anxious to secure on her behalf the prayers of the faithful, which he had been taught from his earliest days to regard as necessary to procure the release of the soul from the purifying flames of purgatory, through which it was supposed it must pass on its way to perfect bliss. These Memorials bore on their very front the earnest petition "*Ora pro anima*" (pray for her soul), and the statues of the deceased queen were placed in a conspicuous position, not only to keep her good name in remembrance, but also that they might, as it were,

* Archæological Journal, vol. XXIX.

appeal silently to the faithful for their prayers on her behalf. With the same object in view, the King also established and endowed chantries at Herdeby, where his consort died, and at other sacred places, where her body rested on its way to the tomb at Westminster. Fragments of Purbeck marble were discovered, during recent excavations, near the Memorial at Waltham, and are supposed to indicate the existence of a Chapel of this description, where, for 250 years, masses were constantly said and prayers offered for the repose of Eleanor's soul. The suppression of Chantries by Edward VI. will account for the disappearance of this building. The King also gave alms to the poor, to secure the repose of the soul of his deceased consort, in accordance with the religious belief of that age. A periodical distribution appears to have taken place on the steps of the Crosses at Waltham and elsewhere, until the suppression of the Chantries. It is stated that the land given by the King for this purpose yielded a clear income of £200 per annum, a sum equal to £2,000 in these days. It is also said that the grand total of £6,250 was expended by the monarch in his desire to perpetuate the memory of his *chere reyne* (dear queen), and this sum was

chiefly spent on the erection of the Memorial
Crosses.   As various amounts were entered in the
Accounts of the Queen's Executors, it has been
supposed that the King's Exchequer was not
impoverished by the outlay, but that the Queen's
money was used for the purpose.

The number of Eleanor Memorial Crosses
erected by Edward I., has been variously stated,
but, from a comparision of the lists given in the
Royal Accounts and in the works of eminent
writers, it seems that twelve places, at least, were
selected for this mark of royal favour, namely,
Lincoln, Grantham, Stamford, Geddington, Northampton, Stoney Stratford, Woburn, Dunstable,
St. Albans, Waltham, Westchepe or Cheapside,
and the village of Cherrynge or Charing, near
Westminster.   Three of these monuments only
have survived the ravages of the past, and are
still standing on the sites assigned to them six
centuries ago, at Waltham, Geddington, and
Northampton.   The Cross at Waltham has also
retained its position as the most elegant and
best preserved of the existing Memorials of the
good and faithful Queen.   It was erected in the
centre of a triangular green, at the point where
the funeral procession diverged from the high

road, on its way from St. Albans to the famous
Abbey Church of Waltham Holy Cross, which
is situated in the adjoining county of Essex,
about a mile to the east of the Eleanor Memorial. The mourners stayed with their dead at
Waltham Abbey, during the night of Dec. 13th,
1290, and early the next day retraced their steps to
the site marked out for the Cross, on their way to
Westminster, where the interment took place
on Dec. 17th. Gough, the learned author of
"Sepulchral Monuments," thinks it strange that
the procession should have turned aside from the
direct route to pass a night at Waltham, when it
was so near the Metropolis. It must, however,
be remembered, that, although its ancient glory
has long since departed from Waltham Abbey, it
was in high repute in ancient times, both with
king and people, and became the popular resort
of pilgrims and the devout in the vicinity of
London. It was in a double sense a royal
foundation, having been founded first as a
Minster or Collegiate Church by King Harold II.,
whose royal tomb was in existence before the
high altar at the time of Queen Eleanor's funeral,
and the heroism and patriotism of the last of the
Saxon kings must have won the sympathy and

admiration of the great warrior, King Edward I. It had, moreover, been raised to the dignity of an Abbey by the monarch's own ancestor, Henry II., and its Abbot was one of the most wealthy and powerful peers of the realm. The King had also become greatly attached to Waltham Abbey, and had spent many pleasant hours with his beloved consort under the shadow of its venerable walls. Beside all this, it afforded the only suitable resting-place that could be found near London, the distance from St. Albans being too great to allow of that early entrance into the Metropolis, which was necessary, on account of the large concourse of nobles and prelates, clergy and people, who desired to meet it at the gates of the city. It is not at all strange then that the body of Queen Eleanor should have been brought to rest for a night near Harold's tomb, just as seventeen years later the remains of her royal husband found a temporary resting-place in the same venerable house for the space of three months, and so was kept above ground until the war with the Scots was concluded, in accordance with his dying command.

The beautiful Memorials of the tender affection of King Edward for his deceased queen belong rather to the Decorated style than to the Early English which followed it. It is true, however, that whilst the Crosses of Waltham and Northampton are peculiarly rich and of elegant composition, the Memorial at Geddington, which is of later date, is comparatively plain. The armorial bearings and achievements of the queen as the wife of the King of England, and the daughter of Ferdinand III., King of Spain, occupy a conspicuous place in each cross. Her statues were placed on the monuments in niches and under canopies. These figures, of which there are three at Waltham, were designed by William Torel, or Torelli, and carved by Alexander of Abington, Dymenge de Legeri and William de Hibernia, *Imaginatores*, image makers or sculptors. It is thought by Gough that not only the statues, but the Crosses also, were copied from the designs of Torel, who must have been a man of genius. He was a London goldsmith of great renown during this reign, and is supposed to have been a native of Italy. His name frequently occurs in the Royal accounts, in connection with the work of raising the Crosses. The Memorials at Waltham, Geddington, and Northampton have been attributed by Vertue and Walpole to the famous Roman sculptor, Pietro Cavalini, who is noted for his mosaic work in the porch of St. Peter's at Rome, but their theory lacks the support of sufficient evidence. The name of this sculptor is not once mentioned in the Royal accounts, and it is said that he was only eleven years old when Queen Eleanor died.

Waltham Cross was commenced early in 1291, and was not finished until Michaelmas, 1292, as the last payment for labour in connection with it was made during that term. It is hexagonal in form, and consists of three elegantly constructed storeys or compartments, decreasing progressively at every stage. Each division is finished by an embattled frieze or cornice, and at every angle is a graduated buttress, ornamented with foliated crockets and finials. Within the panelled tracery of the lower storey are the shields of England, Castile and Leon, and Ponthieu. The three graceful statues of the Queen enrich the open divisions of the second storey, which is the most elegant portion of the structure. The principal person engaged in the erection of the Cross was Dymenge de Legeri (Dominic of Leger) or, as he is named in one of the entries, Nicholas Dymenge de Reyns or Reims. His chief assistants were Roger de Crundale, who afterwards completed his brother Richard's work at Charing Cross ; Alexander de Abington, sculptor ; and Robert de Corfe, who supplied the capital. Dymenge and Alexander were also associates in the construction of the monument of Queen Eleanor in Lincoln Minster. Dymenge was probably a Frenchman, or an Italian, whilst his colleague appears to have been an Englishman. Other names are mentioned in the Royal accounts in connection with the work at Waltham, and among these appear the following :—Richard de Crundale, the builder of the original Charing Cross, which was destroyed by Cromwell's soldiers ; Roger de Walecote, who seems to have served as one of Eleanor's bailiffs ; and Moses of Waltham, probably of Jewish descent, and a resident in the adjoining parish of Waltham Abbey. A family of that name had settled in that town as early as the year 1189, more than a century before the erection of the Cross. Henry Mauger and Richard de Blund or Blount are also mentioned, the first-named having received payment for a supply of "*petra de kam*" (caen stone). The other materials used were Sussex and Purbeck marble. The decorated parts of the monument were made in

10

London, and then sent to Waltham. The cost of the Cross is given at £95, which is equivalent to the modern sum of £1,000, an amount exceeding that expended on others at a greater distance from London, showing that it was richer in details. The King was, no doubt, anxious that the Memorials of his *chere reyne* in or near the Metropolis should excel, in workmanship and general design, the monuments erected in the Provinces, as these would be continually before his eyes, and under the observation of his courtiers and leading citizens. Thus the architecture of the Crosses at Waltham, Westchepe, and Charing was of a higher order, and the ornamentation more elegant than could be found elsewhere.

Waltham Cross, like the Eleanor Memorials at Northampton and Geddington, has been providentially preserved from the destruction which befell the remainder of the monuments of King Edward's piety and affection. It lost its Chantry and the endowments, which made provision for memorial services for the dead, and alms for distribution among the poor, but in other respects it suffered little, except from the injury wrought by the ravages of time and weather. It is a remarkable fact that it was left unmolested by Cromwell's

Ironsides and Iconoclasts, when they marched past
on their way to the Abbey Church of Waltham
Holy Cross in 1642, where, in their misguided
zeal, they sacrilegiously entered that venerable
house of God, defacing the monuments, destroying
an old painted window because it displayed a
picture of King Harold which they considered
idolatrous,* and mutilating three of the Service
Books of the Reformed Church of England as
tending to superstition.   It is most likely, however,
that they found public opinion in the neighbourhood too strong to allow of their wreaking their
vengeance on this Memorial, as they had done on
the Crosses in London and at other places.
Reverence for the memory of the good Queen,
who had been so well known and loved by their
ancestors, had not died out among the people in
this locality, and we are probably indebted to them
for the preservation of this national monument in
those troublous times.   The Cross appears to
have suffered more from neglect and injudicious
repairs than from the hand of time or exposure to
the weather.   After the destruction of the ancient
Chantry, the roadway on the south-east of the
Cross was obstructed by the erection of the old

* Fuller's History of Waltham Abbey, ch. 1.

Falcon Inn, which partially obscured that portion
of the monument. The first repairs on record
were undertaken in 1720 and 1757, but these were
of a most trivial character. In 1720 some posts
were presented by the Society of Antiquaries for
the purpose of protecting the Memorial. It is
interesting to notice here that an engraving of the
Cross made in 1718 gives the following dimensions of this ancient monument:—The height,
from the base to the top of the spire, forty feet;
from the ground to the pinnacles of the second
storey, twenty-eight feet; to the tabernacle, twenty
feet; and to the extreme height of the first storey,
fifteen feet. In 1759 the original steps were taken
away, and the base was formed of brickwork.
Dr. Stukely, the learned Secretary of the Society
of Antiquaries at this time, states that the base
was originally surrounded by ten steps, but other
authorities mention six, seven, or eight as the
more probable number. These steps were eventually reduced to *three*, but during the last
restoration the number was again raised to *six*.

In 1795 an ill-advised attempt was made by Sir
George William Prescott, Bart., Lord of the
Manor of Cheshunt, to remove the Cross into his
grounds at Theobald's Park, a short distance on

the north-west of the site which it had occupied
for five hundred years. This undertaking, most
happily, could not be carried into effect, for after
removing the upper tiers of stones, the workmen
found it too hazardous to proceed with their task,
on account of the decayed state of the ornamental
parts. On this occasion, therefore, the damage
caused by the attempt was simply repaired, and
the Cross left in its ruinous condition. In 1832 a
restoration was inaugurated by Mr. W. B. Clarke,
architect, who most generously gave both time
and services to the good work, without fee or
reward. This restoration was carried out before
the end of 1834 at a cost of £1,200, the result of
an appeal to the public. The two upper storeys
of the monument were renewed, but, unfortunately,
not with the best stone ; the lower divisions were
faced where it was found requisite, and iron rails
were placed round the base to protect the Cross.
The late Queen Adelaide defrayed the cost of
restoring the three statues of Eleanor.

Fifty years later, in 1885, another restoration
was deemed essential for the due preservation of
the Memorial. An influential committee was
formed under the presidency of Sir Henry Bruce
Meux, Bart., of Theobald's Park. Mr. Harry

Hems, the well-known sculptor, of Exeter, was appointed to carry out the work under the direction of the architect, Mr. C. E. Ponting, of Lockeridge, Marlborough, Wilts. The restoration, which dealt especially with the second and third stages, proceeded slowly through lack of the necessary funds, but it was at length brought to a satisfactory conclusion in 1892, at a cost of £1,130, raised by public subscription, as in 1834. This sum included a donation of £25, received from Her Most Gracious Majesty the Queen, who had inspected the Cross in 1843, in company with her lamented husband, the late Prince Consort. During the work of restoration, through the munificence of Sir H. B. Meux, the obstruction on the south-east of the Cross was removed, by the demolition of the old Falcon Inn, and the ancient roadway on that side was again opened up to the public. The Cross consequently occupies once more its ancient position in the centre of a triangular space, at the entrance to the road leading to Waltham Abbey, and, as in early days, stands out clearly to view on every side. In laying the foundations of the new Falcon Inn, the workmen discovered the fragments of marble which are supposed to have formed part of the old Chantry.

The concluding portion of the work consisted in the restoration of the six steps at the base of the Cross, and the fixing of new and elegant iron rails round the monument, the lowest step being a facsimile of the bench which still exists underground. This last stage, of a most important work, was most satisfactorily carried out at a cost of £200. The success of the whole undertaking was celebrated by public rejoicings on New Year's Eve, 31st Dec., 1892, when the ancient roadway, newly opened up, was re-dedicated to the public by Lady Meux, and, in honour of the occasion, the ancient custom of distributing alms was revived, her ladyship presenting, from the steps of the Cross, 360 shillings, fresh from the Mint, to the deserving poor of the neighbourhood. The new title of Eleanor Cross Road was also conferred on Waltham Lane, the road on the east of the Memorial, along which the funeral cortege of Queen Eleanor had proceeded to and from the Abbey of Waltham Holy Cross, on its way to the place of interment in the Abbey of Westminster.

Some Hertfordshire Churches.

By A. Whitford Anderson, A.R.I.B.A.

THERE are many remains yet to be found in the churches of Hertfordshire, which take us back in fancy to the so-called "good old days" of the Middle Ages. We can still sit in the porch where our forefathers were married; we can still follow the path of the solemn procession to the churchyard cross on Palm Sunday*; or, should our imaginings take a more gruesome turn by reason of the emblems of mortality spread around us, we might even fancy that the tanned skin of some sacrilegious felon is still nailed to the old door, as sometimes happened in days gone by; or, coming to later times, we can gaze on the old stocks at the entrance to the churchyard, and picture to ourselves some roystering village blade who had not gone to bed betimes, and had found the stocks to be his portion in the morning, while his boon companion of the night before, who, with scarcely less wayward feet, had escaped the village constable, now sits in the churchyard, with his

* R.I.B.A. Sess. Papers, 1867.

head against a tombstone—the coldest one he can find—and ponders. As neither you nor I, reader, can imagine his thoughts upon such an occasion, we shall leave him to his own communings, and examine by ourselves the old church of Brent Pelham, where the stocks still remain at the entrance to the churchyard "to testify to the truth of the story." There are several points of interest about this church. The principal one is an altar tomb under a recess in the north wall, which has given rise to the wildest local traditions. The tomb, which is to some unknown person, bears a figure in relief of an angel bearing to heaven a human soul, in the shape of a small figure. Round the head are the symbols of the four Evangelists, the eagle, the lion, the bull, and the angel, all winged ; while in the centre is a cross-fleurè, with the stem inserted in a dragon's mouth, signifying the triumph of Christianity. The whole, which seems to be not earlier than the thirteenth century, is evidently emblematical of the Resurrection. At some later period, probably post-Reformation, a Latin verse has been added, together with the name Piers Shonkes, and the date, 1086. This being an unknown tomb, it was only natural that the common people should find

a suitable tenant for it. The most popular legend[*]
is that "once upon a time" there lived here a
mighty hunter called Piers Shonkes, who had one
attendant only, and three wonderful winged
hounds, now figured on his tomb (these are the
four Evangelists!) It so happened that Shonkes,
when hunting in the forest, killed a dragon (also
figured on the tomb), which was under the
immediate protection of the Prince of Darkness,
who declared in revenge that he would possess
Shonkes at his death, whether buried within or
without the church. It seems, however, that
Piers was too wily to be caught thus, and left
directions in his will that he should be buried in
the middle of the wall—neither within nor without
the church. His wishes were carried out, and
Shonkes is probably still there guarded by his
huntsman and his faithful hounds.

Another feature of this church is that the
chancel inclines from the nave several degrees to
the north of east. This is said to be a common
feature in Cornish churches, and is supposed to
represent the inclination of our Saviour's head
upon the Cross. In an inventory of the church
furniture, taken in 1297, mention is made of a

* Cussans' History of Hertfordshire.

muscarium, which was a fan used by the deacons for the purpose of keeping the flies off the Eucharist and the persons of the priests.

From Brent Pelham it is but a short distance to Little Hormead, which has a tiny Norman church, chiefly remarkable for some fine Early English wrought iron scroll work on the old door under the built-up Norman doorway on the north side.

Wyddial Church, prettily situated among trees, next claims our attention. Its north chapel is entirely constructed of red brick, with brick internal piers and arches, and brick traceried windows. It was built in 1532 by George Canon, who says in his will, "I bequeathe my soul to Almyghtye God and to oure blyssed Lady Sainte Marye, and to all the company of hevn, and my bodye to be buryed w^{tn} the chapell of Saynte George, in the paryshe church of Wedyall." The chapel is inclosed with old oak side screens, and the contrast of colour between the red brick and the dark oak is refreshing.

Anstey possesses a curious church well worthy of a visit. The churchyard is approached by an old oak lych-gate, with a chamber built of flints beside it. The church itself has a castellated

appearance, due principally to a circular stair
turret, pierced with crenelles, formed like a cross,
as may be seen in many old castles. It is locally
believed that the church was built from the
remains of an old castle which stood hard by, but
the castle was not destroyed until the time of
Henry III., while the greater part of the church
dates from before that period. Some of the old
stones, however, have probably been used in later
additions. Anstey is one of the few cruciform
churches in the county, and has a central tower
resting on Norman arches. The nave arches
have a curious triangular appearance, owing to
the centre from which they are struck being
considerably below the top of the capitals.
Another curious feature is the position of the stair
to the central tower, which, instead of being in or
near one of the tower piers, stands at the south-
west angle of the south transept, so that it required
a gallery round the upper part of the transept to
reach the tower. There are a number of old
stalls with misereres in the chancel, and the
piscina, or water drain, is peculiar as having a
side arch opening upon the adjoining sedilia, or
seat for the priest, thus giving him an unobstructed
view of the High Altar. The font, which seems of

late Norman date, has a square bowl, ornamented
with mermen holding their tails in their hands, in
allusion to baptism by water. Fonts are frequently
found with fish, water, or such subjects sculptured
upon them. Before leaving this church the unique
squints should be noticed. Squints are openings
pierced through an intervening wall to enable
anyone in a side chapel to obtain a view of the
High Altar. In this case the backs of the chancel
piers have been cut away so as to form flying
buttresses behind them, thus giving a wide
opening for those in the transept to see through.

Barkway Church is remarkable for the discovery,
during the restoration in 1862, of a number of
earthenware jars embedded in the chancel walls,
nearly on the floor level. These, examples of
which have been found in other churches, were in
all probability placed there for their acoustical
properties. They were unfortunately broken by
the workmen. Somewhat similar vessels, though
of brass, were noticed by Vitruvius as having been
placed in Roman theatres.

In going from Barkway to our next church at
Ashwell the road through Barley should be taken,
on account of the old-world sign to be seen at the
" Fox and Hounds " Inn there. It stretches from

house to house across the road, and has on it
figures of huntsmen and hounds in full cry after
a fox.

Ashwell Church is undoubtedly the finest in the
county.   It has a lofty Decorated stone tower at
the west end, surmounted by a tall wooden spire
covered with lead.   The tower is the only wholly
stone one in Hertfordshire, but is in a sadly
dilapidated condition, owing to the perishable
nature of the stone employed in its construction.
The spire was re-leaded (perhaps re-built) in 1714
by Thomas Everard, who seems to have waxed so
enthusiastic over his achievement that he felt
compelled to unburden his soul in poetry, which
he has bequeathed to posterity in raised letters
of lead on the roof, as follows :—

> THO. EVERARD
> LAID ME HERE
> HE SAID TO LAST
> AN HUNDRED
> YEAR
> 1714

Then follow a number of names, male and female,
probably the sisters and the cousins and the aunts
whom Thomas had invited to share in his glory
on that elevated spot.   Thomas was, however, a
good craftsman, and did his work honestly and well.
There are a number of remarkable inscriptions in

Latin, evidently cut with a knife, on the inside walls of the tower; one referring to the first great plague in 1349. This church belonged to the Abbey of Westminster, of which Abbey no fewer than twenty-six monks, as well as the Abbot himself, fell victims, and this inscription was probably cut by a survivor. Mr. Cussans* translates the inscription, which is incomplete, as "a mournful pestilence, cruel, deplorable, fierce, and calamitous." There is also a rude sketch, supposed to represent the Abbey Church of Westminster. Immediately below this inscription is another, a later one, recording a furious storm of wind which began on St. Maur's day, 1361. There are many other inscriptions on the columns and other parts of the church, but they are not now legible. There is a fine old open timber lych-gate to the churchyard.

Hinxworth Church has a fine Perpendicular canopied niche in the south-east angle of the nave in what was formerly the Lady Chapel. It is also worthy of note that a low side window opens into this chapel from the churchyard in such a position that no view of the High Altar in the chancel could be obtained through it. The same

* Cussans' History of Hertfordshire.

arrangement, though in a more marked degree, occurs in Wallington Church, and seems to point to the use of those windows as "uttward confessionals."

The finest holy water stoup or basin in the county exists in the north-east angle of the south porch at Caldecot.   It stands under a richly carved and crocketted Perpendicular canopy, the whole being over nine feet in height.   It is curious to find an elaborate piece of work like this in such an out-of-the-way church.   There is no village worthy of the name, and the church stands almost enclosed by a farm-yard, and has a quiet, old-world, dilapidated appearance that would rejoice the hearts of that excellent body of men somewhat flippantly called by their detractors the "Anti-scrape" Society.*   The west tower, like that at Newnham, has small side aisles, which give a picturesque break to the downward lines of the tower.   The Perpendicular font is decorated with shields, that on the west side bearing a Latin cross, with the crown of thorns surmounting a spear and rod in saltire.

Clothall Church is interesting enough to de-

---

* The Society for the Preservation of Ancient Buildings, which has done some excellent service, and if it errs at all it is on the side of safety.

mand attention. The tower, as at Sacombe, stands over the south porch. It is, I believe, however, comparatively modern. There is a south chapel, on the north and south walls of which are the original stone brackets for candles on either side of the altar. There is a good brass here showing the costume of a parson in the time of Elizabeth.

Cottered Church has a large, though much dilapidated, distemper painting on the north wall of the nave. Part of a landscape with a river and small subsidiary figures and buildings are plainly visible, but a large part of the centre is nearly obliterated. Sufficient, however, remains to make it out to be St. Christopher carrying the infant Christ over the river. As there may be some of my readers who are not acquainted with the legend, I shall give it briefly, as it is necessary in order to understand the painting. *Christopher was a heathen giant, who determined to enter into the service of the strongest king he could find. Having found one whom he thought would suit him, he became his servant, and while so engaged he observed that the king invariably crossed himself in fear when-

* From the Golden Legend.

11

ever he heard the devil's name mentioned. Christopher therefore comes to the conclusion that the devil must be a greater man, and at once seeks him out, and transfers his allegiance to him. All goes well for a time, until Christopher begins to notice that the devil trembles when he sees a cross, so he sets out to find the king whose emblem a cross is. In the course of his wanderings he meets a hermit, who instructs him in Christianity, and directs him to use his great strength in carrying travellers across a certain river, and thereby atone for his former sins. One night, when he had been thus employed for some time, he heard a voice calling him from across the river, and upon going out he finds a little child waiting to be carried across. Christopher takes him in his arms, and begins to wade through the river, and as he does so he feels the child growing heavier and heavier, until he was almost more than the giant could bear. On reaching the other side he exclaimed to the child, "You seem to weigh as heavy as the whole world," whereupon the child replied, "Well said, Christopher; I created the world, I redeemed the world, I bear the sins of the world," and immediately disappeared. It was after this that the heathen giant was named Christopherus, or the Christ-bearer. The painting at Cottered adheres very closely to the legend.   The gigantic figure may be dimly made out in the centre of the river ; to the left is a figure, probably the hermit, holding a lantern— for it was night,—while behind him stands a church.   In the foreground is a tiny figure of a man (introduced probably to give scale to the giant) who appears to be fishing in the river. This beautiful legend was a very favourite one with the old painters, and may be found in many churches.

Kelshall is chiefly noted for its unique aumbry, or niche, in the north-west angle of the nave.   It is a tall narrow recess about sixteen feet high, circular on plan, with an internal diameter of two feet six inches.   It had a door at one time, as the marks of the fastenings still exist.   It was probably used as a cupboard for the processional banners used in the church.   The lower part of a church-yard cross, now used as a sundial, still stands in the churchyard on the south side of the church. It is the only example in the county, but all that is left are the three steps and a portion of a plain shaft.

Standon Church, without doubt, presents more

peculiarities than any other church in the county.
The first peculiarity consists in the position of the
tower, which stands to the south of the chancel,
and connected with it by a small chamber only.
This is a unique arrangement in Hertfordshire
and uncommon elsewhere. The only example of
a west porch in this county is also to be found
here. But it is the interior which presents the
greatest features of interest. The floors of both
nave and chancel slope perceptibly upwards from
the west end to the altar, the slope being about
an inch and a half in every seven feet. This has
been supposed to represent our Saviour raised
upon the Cross, but it usually occurs, so far as my
own experience goes, when the church stands on
a slope, or when a vault or crypt has been built
below the chancel, both of which causes exist
at Standon. To obtain a crypt here it was also
necessary to raise the chancel more than usual
above the nave. We have here no fewer than
eight steps up from nave to chancel, and five more
up to the steps of the altar, giving a total rise of
six feet four inches. The view from the west end
looking eastward through the beautiful Early
English chancel arch is very striking. There is a
curious late Norman font here, with an octagonal

bowl of coarse stone, round which is twined, irrespective of the angles, some simple but characteristic foliage. On the south wall of the chancel is an elaborate Elizabethan monument to Sir Ralph Sadleir, the famous statesman and ambassador to Scotland, during the reigns of Henry VIII., Edward VI., the Bloody Mary, and Elizabeth. Beside the monument may be seen a standard said to have been captured by Sir Ralph in person at the battle of Pinkie, where it is said that the English victory was in great measure due to him for rallying the broken English ranks after the first attack by the Scots.

The most interesting points about Little Munden Church are the two altar tombs, with effigies, under the elaborately ornamented arches which separate the chancel from its north chapel. The easternmost tomb, on which are effigies of a man and his wife, the former in plate armour, is supposed to be in memory of Philip Thornbury, a lord of the manor, in the beginning of the fifteenth century. The other tomb is to another member of the same family, the male figure being clothed in plain plate armour, and his lady in a tight-fitting gown. There are three curious little Perpendicular niches on the faces of the octagonal north chancel pier, which formerly contained images, and at the west end of the church is a huge old private family pew, set high up as a gallery, with a stair for access. It is as large as a small sleeping apartment, and was probably frequently used as such, the sides being too high to admit of the smaller members of the family seeing into the church at all. It seems only to want a fireplace.

Graveley Church has a curious double piscina or water drain in the chancel, with characteristic Norman interlacing arches. Judging from the detail, however, it seems to me to belong to the thirteenth century, or Early English period. Walcott[*] tells us that it was not until the thirteenth century that double piscinæ came into use; one basin in which to rinse the holy vessels, and from which the priest was expected to drink, and one in which to wash his own hands. After the thirteenth century, the priests appear to have become less fastidious as to their drink, and one basin only was provided as before. If the example at Graveley be twelfth century work, which I much doubt, it must be a peculiarly early example of the double arrangement.

[*] Church and Conventual Arrangement.

Hitchin Church, in spite of the dreary appearance it presents externally, owing to its walls having been plastered, should on no account be missed. It contains some of the finest woodwork in the county, in the beautiful old traceried screens enclosing the north and south chancel chapels, and also some old carved roofs. The church was rebuilt in the early part of the fifteenth century. There are a number of good tombs and brasses, and an elaborate fifteenth century font, much mutilated, with figures of the twelve apostles round its sides. The church possessed a fine south porch at the beginning of this century, but unhappily the upper part has been removed, the lower portion, however, still remains with its groined stone roof. It may be interesting to mention that the manor of Hitchin at one time belonged to John de Balliol, afterwards a temporary King of Scotland, and the town itself was the residence of such celebrities as the poet Chapman, "the learned shepheard of faire Hitching Hill," Henry Bessemer, and Eugene Aram.

Wheathampstead has a most interesting cruciform church. This church and that at Flamstead are the only two which still retain their

original vestries, both are on the north side of
the chancel, and both were originally of two
stories, the lower one having been used as a
chapel, while the chamber over was probably the
abode of the anchorite, who watched the church
during the night, and who was bound never to
leave the church day or night while under his
vows. Sometimes the recluse was an anchoress,
as we read of an anchoress being admitted to
St. Peter's Church, St. Albans, in 1480. It is
probable that the chamber frequently found
over the porch was used as an abode for an
anchorite. When the anchorite was a priest, as
was usually the case, he would be able to hear
confessions when the church was closed, through
the "low side window," one of which exists in the
chancel at Wheathampstead, and other examples
at Hinxworth and Wallington have already been
referred to. There is a fine canopied piscina in
the chancel here, and in the north transept there
is an elaborately carved reredos, marking the site
of a former chapel altar. One of the chancel
windows has its tracery curiously worked in
the form of a cross.

St. Michael's Church, St. Albans, standing on
the site of ancient Verulam, is a favourite haunt

of the modern pilgrim to see the famous statue of Sir Francis Bacon, sitting in his robes of office as Lord Chancellor, which is placed in a niche in the north wall. But to the lover of old churches this is not the most important feature in the church. Its architecture shows a variety of styles, from Early Norman—some say Saxon, but I can find no evidence for this—up to comparatively modern times. Unfortunately its old, though somewhat dilapidated, western tower, which had been built within the remains of a still more ancient one, has recently been demolished, and a new one erected at another part of the church. This tower so— I must say—wantonly destroyed was one of the most beautiful bits of old weatherbeaten colouring in the county. There is a particularly fine oak Jacobean pulpit, with a canopy, in this church, and fixed to it is the only original iron bracket for the old hour glass in any parish church in Hertfordshire. Another, however, of plainer character is preserved in the vestry at Sacombe.

St. Stephen's Church, St. Albans, is another of the three St. Albans churches founded in the tenth century by Ulsinus, the sixth Abbot, one to St. Peter, the foremost Apostle; one to St. Michael, the chief Angel; and this one to St.

Stephen, the first Martyr.   The chancel of this
church points almost due south-east, towards the
point on which the sun rises on December 26th
(St. Stephen's Day), and this has been adduced
as a proof of the method in which the ancients
set out their churches; this theory, however, is
discounted by the fact that the two other churches,
as well as the Abbey Church itself, point in a
similar direction.   The most interesting object in
this church is the old brass eagle lectern, which
was discovered about the year 1750 buried under
the chancel, where it had doubtless been placed
for preservation during the Civil Wars.   It
bears the name in old characters of "𝕲𝖊𝖔𝖗𝖌𝖎𝖚𝖘
𝕮𝖗𝖎𝖈𝖍𝖙𝖔𝖚𝖓 𝕰𝖕𝖎𝖘𝖈𝖔𝖕𝖚𝖘 𝕯𝖚𝖓𝖐𝖊𝖑𝖉𝖊𝖓𝖘𝖎𝖘." together
with the Scottish Lion rampant and a Bishop's
mitre.   This George Chrichton was Bishop of
Dunkeld (1527-1543), but was previously Abbot
of Holyrood, in Edinburgh, and he appears to
have presented this lectern to the Abbey.   It is
supposed to have been stolen from Holyrood,
during the Earl of Hertford's unexpected attack
on Edinburgh, in 1544.   Sir Ralph Sadleir, of
Standon, whom I have previously made mention
of, accompanied the expedition, and so also did
Sir Richard Lee, of Sopwell, in St. Stephen's

parish, who is known to have brought back the Scottish royal baptismal font, afterwards destroyed during the Civil Wars ; and it seems also probable that he brought back the lectern, and presented it to his own church.

On one of the nave piers may be seen, roughly incised in the stone, the words "*Adveniat R*" (may the King come). This was probably done by one of the many Royalist prisoners confined in this and other Hertfordshire churches, when Fairfax came back to his headquarters in St. Albans, after his capture of Colchester, in 1648.

North Mimms Church is a beautiful example of pure fourteenth century work, and has a fine west doorway covered with characteristic Decorated "ball-flower" ornament ; there is also some excellent tracery in the windows, and some fragments of old stained glass. In this church, as at Sawbridgeworth, stands an old oak communion table with carved legs, of the time of Archbishop Laud. The form of the table is nearly square, so that the priest could stand, as directed in the rubric, at the north *side* of the table, and not merely at the *end*, as was necessary with an altar-shaped table. There are some excellent brasses now affixed to the walls of the chancel. One in particular, representing an unknown man and his wife, has the man's armour beautifully damascened, though now considerably worn, and the lady's figure is peculiar in showing an enormous height from her waist downwards, in comparison with the upper part of her body.

Hemel Hempstead Church is one of the best examples of Norman work in the county. It has a fine Norman central tower, with a lofty timber spire, and the west doorway is a particularly good example of the period. The chancel is covered with the original stone groined roof. The transepts stand three steps higher than the nave, which is a rather unusual feature. On the floor of the old vaulted chamber, on the north side of the chancel, may be seen the remains of a long narrow slab bearing the following curious inscription—

HEERE LVETH INTERRED
THE BODY OF THOMAS DEA
CON THE SONNE OF THOMAS
DEACON AND MARTHA HIS
WIFE OF CORNERHALL BAT
CHELOR OF ARTES AND ST
UDENT IN PHISICK WHO BY
HIS EXTRAORDINARY SPARE
BODY IN RESPECT OF BREAD
TH BEING LONG SICK OF A
CONSUMPTION AND OF HIS
AS EXTRAORDINARY HEIG

HT BEING IN PROPORTION TO
THE LENGTH OF THIS STONE
MIGHT SHEW THE DESIRE HE
HAD TO HEAVEN AND SO DEP
ARTED SEPT. 28 AN. DO. 16—

Great Gaddesden Church is chiefly remarkable for the beautiful Early English foliage carved on the capitals of the nave piers.

Northchurch is connected with a curious being called Peter the wild Boy, who is buried in the churchyard, and commemorated in the church by a fine brass with engraved head after Bartolozzi. Peter was found in the year 1724, in the act of sucking a cow, on a farm in Hanover, and became a protege of George I. He was a perfectly harmless idiot, and could never be taught to speak all his life. He was placed in a farm near Northchurch, in which parish he stayed until his death in 1785. He used to wander about a great deal, and to insure his safe return, he wore a leather collar marked " Peter the Wild Man from Hanover, whoever will bring him to Mr. Fenn, at Berkhamsted, Hertfordshire, shall be paid for their trouble." Music was the only thing that made any impression on him. In the Vestry, at Northchurch, may be seen a very fine oak chest, said to be of Spanish workmanship.

Tring Church has some very curious grotesque sculptured corbels supporting the nave roof, showing the hatred felt by the Regular Clergy towards the Friars. One corbel represents a pig with a friar's cowl; another a fox running off with a goose, an allusion to the wily friar; a third represents a monkey dressed as a friar, with a book in one hand and a bottle in the other.

The church at Sarratt is a small Norman building having a west tower with a saddle-back roof, which is the only example we have of such a roof in this county. It has a further peculiarity that the tower roof runs north and south instead of being in a line with the nave roof as in the case elsewhere. In the north wall of the chancel is a niche which may have been used as an Easter Sepulchre, as among the furniture mentioned as belonging to this church in the time of Edward VI. is the following :—

"It^{m.} a clothe for the sepulchre of yallow silke popingey."

The pulpit here is of Jacobean date, and is of singularly small dimensions.

There are many other items of interest to be found in the churches of Hertfordshire, but as space forbids their enumeration, the seeker after "the long ago" cannot do better than visit the churches personally, and he will be astonished at the beauty of some of the remains, particularly inside the churches, as owing to the local materials out of which they were constructed, many of them are dreary and colourless externally.

I shall close this chapter with a quaint epitaph copied from the churchyard at Shenley:—

"Silent in dust lies mouldering here
A Parish Clerk of voice most clear.
None Joseph Rogers could excel,
In laying bricks, or singing well.
Though snapp'd his line, laid by his rod,
We build for him our hopes in God."

The Two Battles of St. Albans:

I. May 23rd. 1455 ; II. February 17th, 1461.

By Edward Lamplough.

THE deposition of Richard the Second and the accession of Henry of Lancaster, although enacted under the authority of Parliament, and endorsed of the nation, by its interference with the hereditary line of succession made an after revolution possible, if not probable.

In the course of time, when Henry VI. reigned, and the nation was, from various causes, deeply exasperated, the deadly feud between the Dukes of York and Somerset armed the great feudatories of the Crown, and the quarrel almost immediately resolved itself into a strife of dynasties.

Previous to the birth of the Prince of Wales the Duke of York had been regarded as the heir-apparent to the Crown, nor did that event entirely dash his hopes, but rather forced his pretentions to a more active development.

In the year 1454, while Henry was incapacitated by "a violent distemper which affected his mind as well as his body," the Duke of York was

appointed Protector of the Realm.   Somerset had
been arrested and committed to the Tower, and
York deprived him of the government of Calais,
and assumed that important office himself.   The
first steps were taken towards the impeachment of
Somerset; but the proceedings languished, and
the King, recovering his health, resumed his
authority, when Somerset was restored to freedom.   Naturally the Duke complained that
advantage had been taken of an unsustained
charge to deprive him of an important office.
Henry, anxious to prevent hostilities, himself
assumed the government of Calais.

Deeply incensed, York retired into Wales to
raise troops.   The Earls of Salisbury and Warwick joined him, and he marched upon London at
the head of a considerable army.   It was the
second time the Duke had assumed arms against
the King, and the power of the three barons was
so formidable, and the conjunction of circumstances
so favourable to their schemes, that a more warlike prince than Henry might have declined the
conflict and appealed to Parliament.   He, however, showed no hesitation, but raised his
standard, and marched out of London to accept
battle.   Under the Royal Standard rode the

Dukes of Somerset and Buckingham, the Earls of Northumberland, Pembroke, Devonshire, Stafford, Wiltshire, and Dorset, with many knights and gentlemen.   He was reinforced at St. Albans, the scene of the battle, his whole force amounting to about 2,000 men.

A letter addressed to His Majesty by the leaders of the Yorkists is said to have been intercepted; but Henry dispatched the Duke of Buckingham to their headquarters to ascertain their intentions, which were given in the following terms :—" Please it your Majesty Royal to deliver up such as we will accuse, and they to have like as they deserved.   And this done, you to be honourably worshipped as a most rightful king. We will not now slack for no such promise nor oath, until we have them, which have deserved death ; or else we, therefore, to die."

Henry's reply was to charge and command the army of York to disperse, with the threat of the extreme penalty of hanging, drawing, and quartering if they dared to resist him in the field.   He added that he would sooner die that day than surrender any lord that was with him.

The King's army was about to resume its march on the 23rd of May, when the hills com-

manding their line of march were found to be
occupied by the troops of York, to the number
of 3,000.   The Royalists withdrew into St.
Albans, and prepared to maintain its narrow
streets and strong defences against the enemy.

Clifford held the barriers, and conducted the
defence, assisted by Somerset, Buckingham,
Northumberland, and Stafford.   The Yorkists
poured in their arrows with deadly effect, while
the men-at-arms, pikemen, and billmen resolutely
maintained the attack and defence of the barriers.
The Duke of York acted the part of a good
general, and " placed himself upon a rising
ground, from whence he observed all occurrences,
and sent fresh soldiers to supply the places of
such as were slain or wounded."   Warwick
attacked under cover of some gardens, that
formed the weakest point of defence, and charged
through the barriers, bearing all before him.
The slain appear to have chiefly met their death
by the arrows of the archers, although "every man
fought with as much fierceness as if they had
taken up a resolution that not a man in the whole
field should have survived the battle."   Clifford,
Somerset, and Northumberland fell in the King's
defence, with about 120 men ; and the King was

wounded in the face.   Buckingham, Stafford,
Dorset, Wiltshire, and Sudeley were also among
the wounded.   Abbot Wheathamstead saw " here
one lying with his brains dashed out, here another
without his arm ; some with arrows in their
throats, others pierced in their chests."   The
archers appear to have decided the battle, and
York was probably the strongest in this arm.
His own army did not suffer very severely.

The following quaint account of the battle is
given in the *English Chronicle*, published by the
Camden Society in 1856 :—" Thanne came the
kyng oute of the abbey wyth his baner dysplayed
into the same strete, and duke Edmond wythe
hym, and the duk of Bokyngham, the erle of
Northumbrelonde, and the lorde Clyfforde, and
the lorde Sudeley beryng the kynges baner ; and
there was a sore fyghte, as for the tyme, and there
at laste was slayne the sayde duke Edmond, the
erle of Northumbrelond, and the lorde Clyfforde."

The battle was evidently fought on the simplest
lines, and was chiefly remarkable for the gallantry
undoubtedly displayed by both armies.   The
Royalists made a tenacious defence of the barriers
under a heavy hail of arrows, and the Yorkists as
fiercely attacked under cover of their archers, the

decisive movement being that of Warwick, when he took the Royalists in the rear by charging over the gardens.

A nominal pacification of the nation followed, York being reinstated as Protector, but the nobility gradually formed into two parties, and the Wars of the Roses were inaugurated.

York assumed arms in September, 1459, and Salisbury defeated Lord Audley on Bloreheath. The Royalists lost 2,400 men, including Audley and the following knights, Thomas Dutton, John Dunne, Hugh Venables, Richard Molineaux, and John Leigh.

Henry and York met at Ludlow, and a sanguinary battle was imminent, when Sir Andrew Trollop carried his command over to the king, and the Yorkists, panic-stricken, dispersed. The chief leaders took refuge in Calais, and were attainted of treason by Parliament.

On June the 5th, 1460, Salisbury and Warwick landed at Sandwich, and reached London at the head of 25,000 men. The battle of Northampton followed on the 19th of July, when the treachery of Lord Grey of Ruthin gave the victory to York. Henry was captured, and Margaret, the Prince of Wales, and Somerset took refuge in Scotland.

York's claim to the throne was dealt with, and he was declared heir-apparent on November 9th, with the present title of Lord Protector, the succession of the King's son being thus cut off. The Lancastrians in the north flew to arms, and York, somewhat hastily, marched into Yorkshire, where he was compelled to take refuge in Sandal Castle, which Lord Clifford blockaded with a considerable force.   On December the 30th, the Duke of York sallied out with the flower of his chivalry, was surrounded by his enemies, and slain, with his son, the Earl of Rutland, and many valiant knights.   The Earl of Salisbury was captured, and executed at Pontefract.

The ducal coronet of York fell to his son Edward, Earl of March, and became at once a royal crown.   Undismayed by the death of his father, the young Earl marched with his forces to dispute the Lancastrian advance upon the capital. Jasper Tudor, Earl of Pembroke, hung upon his rear with a tumultuary army of Welsh and Irish troops ; upon whom he turned fiercely at Mortimer's Cross, on February 2nd, 1461, put 3,800 men to the sword, and at Hereford hewed off the heads of Owen Tudor, Sir John Throckmorton, and eight of the Lancastrian's captains.

He was proclaimed king, under the title of Edward IV., at London, on the 4th of March. On the 29th of March he secured the crown firmly upon his brows by defeating the Lancastrians at Towton, near York, with dreadful effusion of blood.

In the meantime the second battle of St. Albans had been fought. Wyrcester thus describes the events that led up to it :—" After the battle of Wakefield, Queen Margaret came out of Scotland to York, where it was decided by the Council of the Lords to proceed to London and to liberate King Henry out of the hands of his enemies by force of arms. Shortly after the Feast of the Purification, the Queen, the Prince of Wales, the Dukes of Exeter and Somerset, the Earls of Northumberland, Devonshire, and Shrewsbury, the Lords Roos, Grey of Codnor, Fitzhugh, Graystock, Welles and Willoughby, and many others, amounting in all to 24,000 men, advanced upon St. Albans, and at Dunstable destroyed Sir Edward Poyning and 200 foot."

Margaret's army consisted of English, Irish, Welsh, and Scotch troops, and their excesses tended to the ruin of the Lancastrian cause.

The armies joined battle on February 17th,
1461. The northern army attacked Warwick
fiercely at St. Albans Cross, but his famous
archers checked their advance by pouring in
deadly flights of arrows, and compelled them to
give ground. They were not, however, to be
denied, but fell on again, with invincible courage,
and hewed a bloody pathway through St. Peter's
Street. Fiercely disputing their advance, the
Yorkists fell back, until they concentrated their
forces on the heath at the north end of the town,
when the engagement assumed a more regular
form, as the troops dressed their ranks, and
fought steadily at close quarters. The great
Warwick made a valiant fight, and some measure
of success rewarded his efforts against the wild
fighters of Margaret; but Lord Lovelace
unexpectedly drew off the wing under his
command, and the centre, demoralised by this
act of treachery, broke before the furious attacks
of the Lancastrians, and considerable slaughter and
great confusion followed before Warwick succeeded in rallying the flying troops, disengaging
them from their enemies, and effecting an orderly
retreat. Warwick had brought with him to the
field his royal captive, King Henry, who was

thus, by a fortunate and unexpected chance of war restored to freedom, and to his wife and child.

Thus Wyrcester:—"On the Fastday, February 17th, the Battle of St. Albans was fought, from which the Duke of Norfolk, and the Earls of Warwick and Arundell were forced to seek safety in flight. And there the King was recovered from his enemies and the Earl of Montacute, his Chamberlain, taken prisoner. The Prince of Wales came to his father, the King, in his tent, and was knighted by him, after which the Prince knighted the Earl of Shrewsbury, the Lord Roos, and many others. In this field fell no less than 2,000 men, though not in one battle, but in diverse skirmishes, for the country thereabout is covered with wood. On the Queen's side fell James Lutterell and Arnold Hungerford."

Henry's keepers, while in the tents of Warwick, were the Lord Bonvil and the veteran Sir Thomas Kyreil, who, at his solicitations, and under his assurance of protection, remained with him, instead of securing their escape. Margaret re-fused to endorse the King's assurance, and struck off their heads at St. Albans on Ash Wednesday.

Vainly the Abbot of St. Albans besought King Henry to save the town from Margaret's savage and victorious hordes. They claimed the rights of plundering at will south of the Trent. The plunder of St. Albans closed the gates of London against Margaret, and opened them to the Earl of March, and as already related, the battle of Towton withered the laurels won at St. Albans, fixed the crown of England firmly upon the brows of the youthful victor, and drove Margaret, with her husband and son into a painful exile.

The Battle of Barnet:

April 14th, 1471.

THE sanguinary victory of Towton secured
the house of York against the utmost
efforts of the Lancastrians; but Edward IV.,
self-confident, and careless of the friendship of the
king-making Earl of Warwick, offended that
haughty nobleman, and was constrained to feel
the mighty and wide extending power of the
princely house of Neville. By bestowing the
hand of his daughter upon the King's brother,
the Duke of Clarence, Warwick was enabled to
carry out his scheme of revenge with greater
certainty of success, and on the 3rd of October,
1470, Edward was driven into exile, and Warwick
and Clarence brought King Henry out of the
Tower, and in his name ruled the realm. Edward
was too brave and enterprising a man, and too
strong in adherents to his fortunes, to remain long
in exile. He embarked at Flushing on the 2nd
of March, 1471, but was detained by storms until

the 11th, when his little fleet of fourteen vessels
put to sea. He brought up off Cromer on the
evening of the following day, and landed Sir Robert
Chamberlain and other gentlemen to ascertain the
state of the country. Their report proving un-
favourable, he held on for the Humber, and after
encountering stormy weather, reached Spurn, but
with so scattered a fleet that his forces were landed
at various places. Edward disembarked at
Ravenspurn, his brother Gloucester about four
miles higher up the river, and Earl Rivers some
fourteen miles off, at Paull. The King passed
the night at a village near the place of his landing,
either Kilnsea or Easington, and, on his scattered
troops coming in, commenced his march through
Holderness. The priest, John Westerdale, and
Martin de la Mere made hostile demonstration
against him, and the town of Hull closed its gates
and manned its walls to hold him at defiance ; but
Beverley, being defended by open ditches and
gates only, could offer no opposition to his
entrance. On reaching York he was bitterly
disappointed to find himself shut out, but artfully
dissembled, and gave out that he came simply as
the Duke of York, and a loyal subject of King
Henry, in proof of which he wore in his cap the

ostrich feather, the badge of the Lancastrian Prince
of Wales.   Having made oath of his loyalty to
Henry, he was admitted, and confirmed his oath
on the high altar of the Cathedral.   On the
following morning he departed, leaving a garrison
in the city.   The Marquis of Montague, stationed
at Pontefract with a strong force, made no attempt
to cut him off, and a few of his friends began to
assemble round his banner.   No attack being
made upon him as he marched south, men
gathered confidence in his fortunes, and he
entered London in triumph on the 11th of April.
The Archbishop of York, finding resistance vain,
received him with affected pleasure, and delivered
up to him his unfortunate rival, King Henry,
who was straightway committed to the Tower.
On the afternoon he issued forth to give battle to
Warwick, carrying with him his royal captive.
Clarence, forsaking his father-in-law, the Earl of
Warwick, joined his brother with all his following.

The hostile armies converged upon Gladsmuir
Heath, north of the town of Barnet, and the
captains began to dress their lines and prepare for
the desperate and bloody encounter of the morrow.
Edward found that Barnet was occupied by a
number of his bands ; these he collected under his

banner, and carried to the front, to make head against Warwick's adherents, who had formed in considerable numbers under a hedge-side. In his march forward Edward cleared the suburbs of Barnet, and drove Warwick's skirmishers in.

Warwick and Edward were inflamed against each other by a deep sense of injuries, mortifications, and treacherous abandonments, aggravated by the recollections of the friendship and service that had existed in the earlier years of the struggle, when they were firmly united against the Lancastrians. Warwick had struck Edward severely by seducing Clarence, but in this hour of doubt and peril Edward was perhaps repaid by the return of his brother, his forces being augmented thereby and his confidence increased. Warwick was nerved by indignation to mightier efforts to counteract the confederation of his enemies, and was, probably, less disturbed by their added number than by the moral effect of the treachery practised against him. Injured by the inexplicable inactivity of his brother Montague while stationed at Pontefract, he knew too well that his army was disturbed by suspicions of the fidelity of that nobleman, while the Lancastrians arrayed under his standard, witnesses of so many treacheries in the camp of York, might well doubt the honour of their ancient enemies, thus divided, arrayed in arms against each other, and torn or strengthened by the defection of Clarence. Some effort at conciliation was, however, made by Clarence, who, perhaps for the easing of his conscience, communicated with his father-in-law, only to receive the scornful reply: "Go, tell your master that Warwick, true to his word, is a better man than the false and perjured Clarence!"

Edward had from the first aimed at forcing Warwick to give battle before he could concentrate his forces, and on reaching Gladsmuir Heath in the cold, damp mist of the short April afternoon, he pushed his vanguard boldly to the front, and formed his line close to that of Warwick, in readiness to strike fiercely in the early morning, should the enemy attempt to beat a retreat without coming to blows. The King ought to have known the dauntless spirit of his old companion-in-arms too well to fear that he would shun the "communion of swords." During the short hours of that brooding, cheerless night, Warwick's batteries shot out their red tongues of flame, and boomed sullen and ominous, but so close was the vanguard of

York, that the balls passed over, doing no injury, and Edward wisely refrained from answering with his guns, lest he should draw Warwick's fire to its mark.

The number of troops engaged cannot be arrived at with any degree of certainty. Warwick's army was probably inferior in numbers to that of his opponent, but from 30,000 to 40,000 men may have mingled together in deadly strife in the early hours of that long past Easter Sunday.

In the early dawn of the cheerless, foggy morning, the trumpets sounded their shrill notes, the banners were carried forward, and the captains formed their lines to the best of their ability, under the disadvantages of an obscurity that veiled the movements of their enemies. The armies were drawn up somewhat irregularly, Edward's left wing being outflanked by Warwick's right, and his right in turn outflanking Warwick's left, thus the right of each army stretched forward for some distance without an enemy to meet their charge, and, in the obscurity, without being able to take advantage of the peculiarity of their position. The morning was cold and cheerless, and the fog clouded the pomp and chivalry of the two gallant armies, obscuring the gay tints of plumes and standards, scarves and emblazoned surcoats. The glitter and sheen of bristling arms and polished armour were lost in the mist, and with clashing weapons and blare of trumpets the two armies stood opposed in a gloom that was not without an element of poetic justice.

Edward's army was divided into three lines, with a strong reserve. Young Richard of Gloucester led the first line, Edward and the Duke of Clarence the second, and Lord Hastings the third. Edward and Clarence were accompanied by King Henry, thus cruelly exposed "to be shot at" in the ranks of his enemies. The Marquis of Montague and the Earl of Oxford fought the right wing of the opposing army; Warwick and the Duke of Exeter led the left; and the centre, comprising the archers, was under the command of the Duke of Somerset.

Edward had issued orders that no quarter should be given, and, amid the thunder of the cannon and the deadly hail of arrows, the two armies surged forward through the gloom, and fell on furiously, at close quarters, with their

13

terrible offensive arms, their loud war-cries, breathing hate and vengeance, rising shrilly above the clash and clatter of the weapons.

Warwick, as fierce a warrior as Edward, fought on foot, in the front of battle, with splendid courage and ability, and, uniting at once the soldier and the commander, hurled Oxford's division against Edward's left wing, which was broken, and driven off the field in utter rout. Oxford plied spear and sword with such vengeful activity that the panic-stricken Yorkists fled to the capital, throwing the citizens into a firment of fear and apprehension by spreading the report that Edward's army was routed.

Oxford reined in, resisting the temptations of pursuit, and fell back, in good order, to restore Warwick's line of battle; but Edward with his quick soldier's eye, had seen his opportunity, and ordering forward a portion of the reserves, struck Warwick's flank, and restored the battle. At this moment Oxford's troops were falling back, and his badge, a star with streamers, so closely resembled that of Edward's, a sun with rays, that, in the confusion and gloom, a dreadful mistake occurred. Warwick's troops fell upon Oxford's division, which was thrown back upon

Edward's lines, and attacked at once by friends and foes, dispersed in the utmost confusion, with a great outcry of treachery.

The King grasped the position, and pushed forward his army, delivering a brilliant charge along the whole front of the enemy. It was stoutly met, and a murderous conflict was maintained along the line. Warwick, with an energy and spirit that death alone could tame, exerted himself to restore confidence and order in his army, setting the troops a splendid example of personal courage and conduct. Unable to maintain the battle, he died in the press, where the storms raged in its wildest fury. Montague, observing his peril, pushed forward to save or avenge him, but was immediately slain. The last desperate attempt to rally, and stem the tide of Edward's splendid advance, having failed, Warwick's army gave way, and was driven off the field with great slaughter, the victors pressing on in fierce pursuit, and putting the unfortunate fugitives to the sword with the pitiless severity of civil war.

Oxford and Somerset succeeded in making good their escape from the dreadful scene of confusion and slaughter; and Exeter, although severely wounded, and left on the field, was carried off, and found refuge in Westminster. The mangled bodies of Warwick and Montague, after being exposed in St. Paul's for three days, were interred in Bisham Abbey, Berkshire. The Yorkists lost the Lords Cromwell and Say, a son of Lord Montjoy's, and Sir Humphrey Bourchier.

Edward, having spent three hours in warlike toil at Barnet, re-entered London in triumph, and on the afternoon of that red Easter Sunday knelt in prayer in St. Paul's, where he deposited his banner.

An obilisk, erected by Jeremy Sambroke in 1740, distinguishes the scene of this sanguinary conflict. The account of the battle, as given in Warkworth's Chronicle, agrees in its main points with the preceding narrative, the variations referring to the Marquis of Montague's action, and the death of Warwick.

Its inclusion here requires no apology. "Afterward that, he came towards Nottingham, and then came to him Sir William à Stanley, with three hundred men, and Sir William Norris, and divers other men, and tenants of Lord Hastings, so that he had two thousand men and more; and anon after he made his proclamation, and called himself

King Edward of England, and of France. Then
he took his way to Leicester, where were the
Earl of Warwick, and the Lord Marquis, his
brother, with four thousand men or more. And
King Edward sent a messenger to them, that if
they would come out, that he would fight with
them. But the Earl of Warwick had a letter
from the Duke of Clarence, that he should not
fight with him, till he came himself; and all this
was to the destruction of the Earl of Warwick,
as it happened afterwards. Yet so the Earl of
Warwick kept still the gates of the town shut, and
suffered King Edward to pass towards London;
and, a little out of Warwick, met the Duke of
Clarence with King Edward, with seven thousand
men, and there they were made accord, and made
a proclamation forthwith in King Edward's name;
and so all covenants of fidelity made betwixt the
Duke of Clarence and the Earl of Warwick,
Queen Margaret, Prince Edward, her son, both
in England, and in France, were clearly broken
and forsaken of the said Duke of Clarence;
(which in conclusion was destructive both to him,
and them; for perjury shall never have better end
without great grace of God. *Vide finem*, etc.).
King Harry then was in London, and the Arch-

bishop of York, within the Bishop of London's palace. And on the Wednesday next before Easterday, King Harry, and the Archbishop of York with him, rode about London, and desired the people to be true unto him; and every man said they would. Nevertheless Urswyke, Recorder of London, and divers Aldermen, such that had rule of the city, commanded all the people, that were in harness, keeping the city, and King Harry, every man to go home to dinner; and in dinner-time King Edward was let in, and so went forth to the Bishop of London's palace, and there took King Harry, and the Archbishop of York, and put them in ward, the Thursday next before Easterday. And the Archbishop of Canterbury, the Earl of Essex, the Lord Berners, and such others as owed King Edward good will, as well in London, as in other places, made as many men as they might, in strengthening the said King Edward; so then he was a seven thousand men strong, and there they refreshed well themselves, all that day, and Good Friday. And upon Easter Even, he and all his host went towards Barnet, and carried King Harry with them, for he had understanding, that the Earl of Warwick, and the

Duke of Exeter, the Lord Marquis of Montague, the Earl of Oxford, and many other knights, squires, and commoners, to the number of twenty thousand, were gathered together to fight against King Edward. But it happened that he, with his host, were entered into the town of Barnet, before the Earl of Warwick, and his host. And so the Earl of Warwick, and his host, lay without the town all night, and each of them loosed guns at the other all the night. And on Easter-day in the morning, the fourteenth day of April, right early each of them came upon the other; and there was such a great mist, that neither of them might see the other perfectly. There they fought from four of clock in the morning, unto ten of clock in the forenoon. And divers times the Earl of Warwick's party had the victory, and supposed that they had won the field. But it happened so, that the Earl of Oxford's men had upon them their lord's livery, both before and behind, which was much like King Edward's livery, the sun with streams; and the mist was so thick, that a man might not perfectly judge one thing from another; so the Earl of Warwick's men shot and fought against the Earl of Oxford's men, thinking and supposing that they had been King Edward's men; and anon the Earl of Oxford's men cried 'treason! treason!' and fled away from the field with eight hundred men. The Lord Marquis of Montague was agreed, and appointed with King Edward, and put upon him King Edward's livery, and a man of the Earl of Warwick's saw that, and fell upon him and killed him. And when the Earl of Warwick saw his brother dead, and the Earl of Oxford fled, he leaped on horseback, and fled to a wood by the field of Barnet, where was no way forth; and one of King Edward's men had espied him, and one came upon him and killed him, and despoiled him naked. And so King Edward got the field. And there was slain of the Earl of Warwick's party, the Earl himself, Marquis of Montague, Sir William Tyrell, Knight, and many others. The Duke of Exeter fought manfully there that day, and was greatly despoiled and wounded, and left naked for dead in the field, and so lay there from seven of the clock till four in the afternoon, which was taken up and brought to a house by a man of his own, and a leech brought to him, and so afterwards brought into the sanctuary at West-minster. And of King Edward's party was slain

the Lord Cromwell, son and heir to the Earl of
Essex; Lord Berners, his son and heir (Sir
Humphrey Bourchier); Lord Say, and divers
others to the number, of both parties, of 4,000
men. And after that the feud was down, King
Edward commanded both the Earl of Warwick's
body and the Lord Marquis' body to be put in a
cart, and returned himself with all his host again
to London, and there commanded the said two
bodies to be laid in the Church of St. Paul's, on
the pavement, that every man might see them;
and so they lay three or four days, and afterwards
were buried. And King Harry being in the
forward during the battle was not hurt; but he
was brought again to the Tower of London,
there to be kept."

Little more than a fortnight later the battle of
Tewkesbury was fought, when the Lancastrians
were defeated, Margaret of Anjou was captured,
and her son, the young Prince of Wales, slain.
A few weeks more and King Harry died in the
Tower. Then Edward reigned in peace until
death called him away, and Richard of Gloucester
came in, red-handed as his brothers, to end his
life and the Wars of the Roses under Stanley's
spears on Bosworth field, August 22nd, 1485.

The Rye House Plot.

By Thomas Frost.

THE latter years of the reign of Charles II.
offer a striking contrast in the gloom
inspired by a succession of real and pretended
conspiracies and executions for political offences
to the rejoicings and acclamations with which he
was welcomed to the throne. Though the
character of the King was in many respects very
different to that of his father, he was equally
intent upon rendering himself absolute and un-
doing the work of the Reformation. Step after
step in both directions roused the minds which
still cherished ideas of civil and religious freedom
so powerfully that a wide-spread conspiracy was
at length concerted for the dethronement of the
King and the firm establishment of constitutional
government, of which there seemed no hope so
long as the reins were held by either Charles or
his brother. The leaders in this movement were
the Duke of Monmouth, the Earls of Shaftesbury
and Essex, Lord Howard of Escrick, Lord William

Russell, Algernon Sidney, and John Hampden, grandson of the Parliamentary champion of that name who fell, mortally wounded, in the battle of Chalgrave Field. But the aims of these leaders were far from harmonious. Monmouth hoped to have his legitimacy proclaimed, and himself set in the place of his father. Russell and Hampden would have been content with the exclusion of the Duke of York from the throne, and the redress of the nation's grievances. Sidney and Essex cherished the hope of restoring the Commonwealth. Howard probably had no other aim than to serve his own purposes and interests. Shaftesbury dropped out of the plot, and retired to Amsterdam, while it was still in the process of incubation, because he thought his colleagues too cautious.

The design of the conspiracy was formed in 1681, and included a rising in the city of London, where it was regarded with considerable favour, and an insurrection in the western counties, where the Duke of Monmouth had many partisans. Shaftesbury, aided by an Independent minister named Ferguson, was to raise the city, where the latter had considerable influence; and the Earl of Macclesfield, Lord Brundon, Sir William Court-

ney, Sir Francis Knowles, and Sir Francis Drake
undertook the direction of the movement in the
west. The divergence of views among the
conspirators interposed so many delays that
Shaftesbury abandoned the enterprise, which
gradually, owing to the same causes, and to the
unwillingness of Russell to countenance measures
of violence, passed into the hands of a set of
subordinate conspirators, who frequently met
together, and carried on projects unknown to
Monmouth and his colleagues.

These lower grade plotters were Rumsey and
Walcot, who had held colonel's commissions in
the army of the Commonwealth; Goodenough,
the Under-Sheriff of the City of London; Ferguson, who has already been mentioned; and
Rumbold, a farmer, who had served, at an earlier
period of his life, in the ranks of the Parliamentary
forces. Rumsey and Ferguson were the only
members of this secondary council who had access
to the leaders. According to the revelations made
by the men who betrayed the conspirators to the
ruling powers, and the evidence given on the trial
of those who were in consequence arrested, their
object was to waylay and assassinate the King
and the Duke of York on their return from

Newmarket, and then to proclaim the Duke of Monmouth, who, besides being a Protestant, was very popular with all classes of the people.

Rumbold's farm was well situated for the accomplishment of this purpose. The house was on the high road, between Broxbourne and Hoddesdon, and had been built in the fifteenth century by one Andrew Osgard, who received a licence from Henry VI. to construct walls of unusual thickness, and to defend them with battlements and loopholes. It is now in a very dilapidated condition, little more than the walls remaining, these being of red bricks, and the structure one of the earliest of those erected after the form of bricks was changed from the ancient flat and broad kind, such as the Romans made, to the modern shape. Its most prominent features at the present day are the spiral Tudoresque chimneys, which are apt to attract the traveller's attention when journeying on the Great Eastern Railway, or that of the angler who visits the neighbourhood for a day's fishing in the river Lea.

The plan of the conspirators was to stop the progress of the royal carriage by overturning a cart on the road, and to shoot down the King and his brother from the cover of the farm buildings

and walls as they alighted to ascertain the cause
of the stoppage. For this purpose they were said
to have provided themselves with six blunder-
busses, twenty muskets, and twenty or thirty pairs
of pistols, these weapons being described in their
secret communications as swan quills, goose quills,
and crow quills respectively, while powder and
bullets were mentioned under the names of ink
and sand. The purpose of the conspirators was
frustrated, however, by a fire at the house occupied
by Charles and his brother at Newmarket, which
obliged them to leave that town sooner than they
had intended, and consequently before the conspirators were prepared to receive them.

The first hint of the existence of this plot
was received from a man named Keeling, a
wine merchant, who had in some way obtained
a clue, and communicated his knowledge of it
to Lord Dartmouth, but only after the plot had
proved abortive. The immediate consequence
was the arrest of an attorney named West, who
is said to have made a confession, which led
to the arrest of Walcot and Rumbold, that of
Russell, Sidney, Hampden, Essex and Howard
following soon afterwards. Public interest was
much excited by the trials of these alleged

participators in the plot, and especially in those of Russell and Sidney, against whom there was no evidence to connect them with the designs of the Rye House party, which neither of them appear to have known anything about. It was a great point with the promoters of the prosecution to implicate them in the plot, and recourse was had to every conceivable means to obtain evidence against them.

Warrants were issued for the arrest of Monmouth and Lord Grey, but they succeeded in evading the officers of the law, and escaped to the continent. That the warrant was not intended to be executed in the case of Monmouth may readily be believed in view of the fact that he was the King's favourite among his illegitimate sons, and very popular far beyond the court circle. Lord Grey was a man of the worst character in private life. He had been the defendant in one of the most disgraceful trials known in the annals of British jurisprudence, involving the honour of more than one family of the aristocracy ; but he was one of Monmouth's most intimate and trusted friends. It was he who commanded the cavalry in Monmouth's final enterprise, in which his cowardice contributed in no small degree to the loss of the battle of Sedgemoor.

Letters were found in the possession of Walcot and Rumbold which showed that they had been in communication with the leaders in the conspiracy; but the only evidence which could be made to support a charge of treason was contained in the alleged confession of West. Lord Howard, who had betrayed Shaftesbury in 1674, was found willing, however, to act a similar base part in 1683; and, to save his own head from the block, offered himself as a witness for the Crown. The first of the accused brought to trial was Lord William Russell, on the 13th July, the judge being the historically infamous Jeffreys, who a few years later condemned himself to eternal odium by his barbarities and outrageous disregard of both law and decorum, during his judicial campaign in the south-western counties, justly stigmatised as the "Bloody Assize."

Russell objected, counsel for the defence of prisoners not being allowed in those days, that some of the jurors who were to try him were not freeholders; but he was told that the law required juries to be summoned from that class only for the purpose of securing in that capacity men of property, and by presumption, better educated and more intelligent than those in an inferior social position, and that this was unnecessary in Russell's case, as the jury was composed of citizens of London. In fact, it was added, a sufficient number of freeholders to form a jury could not be found, as few of the merchants and tradesmen who lived in the city were of that class. In answer to the application of the accused for notes of the evidence, he was told that no official report would be supplied, but that he could employ a servant to take notes for him. Lady Russell was then allowed to enter the dock, and be seated by her husband's side, where she sat patiently through the trial, intent upon the proceedings and diligently taking notes.

The first witness called was Lord Howard, who stated, with some nervousness of manner, that the directors of the conspiracy were the Duke of Monmouth, the Earl of Essex, Lord William Russell, Algernon Sidney, John Hampden, and himself. At that moment an unusual manifestation of excitement was observed in the crowded court, and one of the officials made some communication in a whisper to the witness, whose voice immediately dropped and faltered so much that he could

14

scarcely be heard. Jeffreys admonished him to
speak louder, and asked the cause of his
agitation.

"An unhappy accident," replied the witness,
"hath just happened that hath sunk my voice."
It then became known that, just as the trial had
commenced, Lord Essex had asked for a razor
that he might shave himself, and entering his
bedroom had cut his throat with so much violence
as to almost separate the head from the body.   A
shudder ran through the court as the dreadful fact
became known, but the trial was proceeded with,
the accused being found guilty, as the court and
the judge intended he should be, and sentenced
to death.

Lady Russell obtained admission to the royal
presence, and made a pathetic appeal to Charles
on her husband's behalf, urging his innocence of
the crime imputed to him, and the loyal services
of her father, Sir Thomas Wriothesley. The
king heard her graciously at first, but, though her
appeal was supported by the prayers of the
Duchess of Portsmouth, the frail Louise de
Querouaille, her importunity soon wearied him,
and he repulsed her at last almost brutally. Lord
Cavendish is said to have proposed to save

Russell from the scaffold by changing clothes
with him, and taking his place in prison ; but the
condemned man refused to abandon his friend to
the tender mercies of the court. The execution
took place on the 21st July, in Lincoln's Inn
Fields.

Sidney was not brought to trial until
November, the jury in his case being chosen
from inhabitants of the county of Middlesex.
Sidney objected that they were not all
freeholders, but Jeffreys overruled the objection,
although the principle had been admitted in
Russell's case, and the reason for allowing
the exception in that case would not have
applied to the county. Jeffreys delivered
this judgment in terms studiously harsh and
vindictive. He hurled the bitterest invectives
against the accused, more like a prosecutor who
was also a political opponent than an impartial
judge ; and throughout the trial strained the law
against him whenever it was doubtful, and made
the most of every point in favour of the Crown.
The chief witness was again Lord Howard, who
now spoke with more confidence, and told his
story more coherently. The law requiring two
witnesses in cases of treason, a political treatise

was put in as a second piece of evidence; and though this was unpublished, and the writing could not be proved to be Sidney's, Jeffreys ruled that it was admissible, on the ground that the views set forth in it might lead to acts such as were charged against the accused. Sidney applied for counsel to argue the point of law involved in this ruling, as counsel were allowed to do, though they might not examine witnesses or address the jury; but Jeffreys refused, saying there was no doubtful point of law in the case. The jury returned a verdict of guilty, and the execution of Sidney followed in due course.

The trial of Hampden came next. As no documentary evidence could be found in his case, the Duke of York endeavoured to induce the Duke of Monmouth (who had been pardoned and allowed to return to Court, on making an abject apology to his father) to corroborate the evidence of Lord Howard; but this, to his credit it must be said, he firmly refused to do, and on being summoned to appear and give evidence, again withdrew to the continent. Hampden escaped, therefore, with a fine of forty thousand pounds. Of the others accused, Rumbold and

Walcot were executed, the former being hanged on a tree near the Rye House ; and the remainder were sentenced to various terms of imprisonment or fined more or less heavily in proportion to their means.

Witchcraft in Hertfordshire.

By Lewis Evans.

DEVILISH apparitions and cases of witchcraft seem to have been fairly numerous
in the county about 200 years ago, and though
we have no very recent records of such things,
and it seems that in spite of the proverb
these wonders at any rate have ceased; still
amongst the printed records of Hertfordshire
there are many cases of the kind which are no
doubt as well authenticated as some other
historical facts. For instance, a rare tract
informs us that in August, 1678, "there hapned
so unusual an Accident in Hartfordshire" as
the following :—A rich industrious farmer, who
had a small crop of about three half acres of
oats ripe, sent to a neighbour to agree with him
about mowing or cutting the oats. The poor man
asked a good round price for his labour, whereupon some sharp words passed and finally, the
irritated farmer with a stern look and hasty gesture
told the poor man, " that the Devil himself should

mow his oats before he should have anything to
do with them," the result of this rash statement
is then described in the following terms. "We
will not attempt to fathom the cause, or reason
of Preternatural events ; but certain we are, as the
most credible and General Relation can inform us,
that that same night this poor mower and farmer
parted, his field of oats was publickly beheld by
several Passengers to be all on a flame, and so
continued for some space, to the great constern-
ation of those that beheld it, which strange news
being by several carried to the farmer next
morning, could not but give him a great curiosity
to go and see what was become of his crops of
oats—the inquisitive farmer no sooner arrived
at the place where his oats grew, but to his
admiration he found the crop was cut down ready
to his hands, and as if the Devil had a mind
to shew his dexterity in the art of husbandry,
and scorn'd to mow them after the usual manner,
he cut them in round circles, and plac't every
straw with that exactness that it would have
taken up above an age for any man to perform
what he did in that one night—and the man
that ows them is as yet afraid to remove them."
The rough woodcut we reproduce clearly shows

the three half acre field with the crop being mown, but unfortunately neither the name of the farmer nor the exact locality is recorded in the four pages on which this history is printed.

The next appearance of the Devil in Hertfordshire seems to have been near Redbourne, shortly before the year 1680, when he appeared to Mr. Michael Beynon in the shape of a lion. Mr. Beynon, who was a popish novice, stayed three nights at an inn near Redbourne, and on the first night at about two o'clock was roused by a very bright and shining light darting itself up and down, to and fro upon the wall, at which sight he arose and went to his accustomed prayers to the Virgin Mary and all the Saints, and the next day gave himself to fasting and prayer, because he thought he had seen an angel to confirm him in his religion. The next night, about three, he felt a heaviness on his breast, and again saw the light on the wall, but being heavy with sleep he turned over and purposed not to mind it, whereupon something smote him with a small blow on the shoulder, and a low voice said "Sleep not." Upon that he sat up in bed, and saw an appearance as it had been of a little child, very beautiful; so he arose and prayed as before, and kept the next

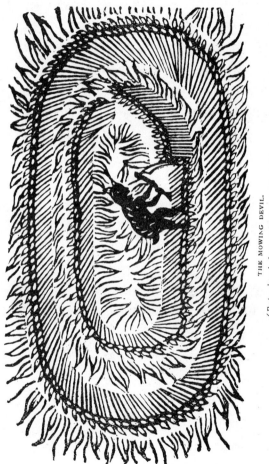

THE MOWING DEVIL.

(*Reproduced from a woodcut of 1678.*)

day very strict in fasting and prayer, and when
night came slept until towards morning, and then
"felt something lye very heavy upon his feet;
now thinking it had been some part of his wearing
clothes, he lift up his feet, and immediately heard
something (as it were) grabble down behind his
beds-head, but, looking, found nothing, but was
again surprised with the light upon the wall,
which strook him with such amazement that he
could get nothing on save his breeches, and so
upon his knees by the beds-side he went to prayer
with his beads in his hand." Then there appeared
to him "a great lion and a chain about him, and
appearances like dogs surrounding of him, and he
thought they would have sucked his breath from
him." When getting no help, in spite of his
prayers, "his heart failed him, and he cried out to
Jesus Christ for help and deliverance, so that after
a little time he had that confidence that he told
the lion (the Devil) that he should have no power
over him." After his deliverance out of the paw
of this lion, he burn'd his pardons and his beads,
and entirely renounced the Church of Rome.
Some people might think that the practical joker
should be called to account for these spiritual
manifestations, or that the whole story had been

invented by some unscrupulous ultra-Protestant ; but the author, in his address to the kind reader, after premising " that our age doth so swarm with lebells of lies, and pamphlets of falsehoods, and fictions of men's brains that it is become a thing next to an impossibility for ought that is strange and miraculous (although truth) to find entertainment amongst men." subjects this relation "into the hands of the diligent inquirer into things to prove and try it, to see whether it be truth or not."   These two are, I believe, the only cases in which the actual appearance of the Devil is recorded in our county, but several cases of demoniacal possession took place in it, as for instance in the deplorable case of the children of John Baldwin of Sarrat, described by T.A. (Aldridge), in the year 1706.   The names of these children were Anne, born 1686 ; Rebecca, 1688 ; and Mary, 1690 ; poor Rebecca was the first victim in 1700, when, after an illness succeeded by fits, etc., she one day began making strange noises, first like a bumble bee, then a kitten, a cat, and then a dog ; and that louder and louder, and continued so doing all night.   After this disastrous beginning she had other fits, and it would be said by her mouth " I'll burn ye," and

then it was hard work to hold her, so as to keep
her out of the fire.   These fits ceased after a time,
apparently under medical treatment, but when
her sister Mary began in 1702 to have fits of
dumbness and blindness—when it would be said
by her mouth "Now she shall be blind"—poor
Rebecca became worse than ever, she and her
sister seeing men and women who were invisible
to others, and having seizures of various kinds,
losing the use of their limbs, only being able to
go backwards, and falling down after due notice
given "Now she shall fall down," and so on.
The manifestations continued for some time, but
in the following year John Baldwin had a series
of prayer meetings at his house on behalf of the
children, who were thereby cured.   Richard
Carter, one of those who assisted, recites the
following particulars of the event : " In the time
of prayer Mary Baldwin was taken very ill; and
after prayer was over it was declared to me by
her, and others who saw it, that towards the end
of that day of prayer Mary was so ill that she
thought she should vomit and went out of the
room, (and her sister Rebecca went out with her)
and Mary cast up (as she thought) a piece of
flesh as big as a mouse, and she said then she see

several of the appearances standing about it and
her, and they said they cou'd not meddle with her
any more, and she said she thought the piece of
flesh crawl'd away, and the appearances went
away with it snivelling and crying." Even after
this merciful deliverance the family had little rest
for a time as Anne, an elder daughter, was
afflicted in a similar way, though she likewise
became cured at a Prayer Meeting towards the
end of 1704.

The following are some of the more ordinary
cases of witchcraft. Mary Hall, a smith's
daughter, at Little Gadsden, in 1664, made
strange noises like to mewing of cats, barking
of dogs, roaring of bears, etc., and was bewitched
by two little imps (Goodwife Harod's and
Young's), who came down the chimney riding
on a stick, and spoke by her mouth in two
different voices, accompanied by strange movements and swelling of the throat, though
sometimes her lips did not move. Elizabeth Day,
of Hitchin, who could run up walls, and from
whose mouth on suffumigation an imp leaped
forth in the shape of a mouse.

The great test for witches was to tie their toes
and thumbs together and duck them in a pond,

when the witches were supposed to float and others to sink. This interesting ordeal by water was often tried in Hertfordshire, two suspected persons were thus tested at Baldock, one of whom sank immediately, but the other could not be made to sink; also a lady nick-named Mary-by-chance could not sink with all the means she could use, though some say she had iron next her to make her sink, and another witch who was ducked at St. Albans could not sink though she strove by putting her head under water, and was thrust down with poles, and confessed that one of her imps leaped upon her breast in the water, and she could not sink. Witchcraft was the cause of several trials at Hertford Assizes, two of which occupied prominent positions in the history of the black art, and it was at one trial at Hertford that a witch before the judge and her accusers once said, " She was sure not to die yet, for all the mischief she had done, was in transforming herself into the shape of a Bumble Bee, and biting the maids' thread often in pieces as she spun."

In 1711, Sir Henry Chauncy, the first historian of Hertfordshire, committed Jane Wenham to Hertford gaol to stand her trial for witchcraft, and by this means called attention to the county much more fully than by his book published eleven years before.   Jane Wenham having been tried on March 4, 1711-12, and contrary to the judge's wishes, convicted, was condemned to death as a witch, and thereupon the whole of England was roused to discussions on the existence or possibility of witches and witchcraft. In Jane Wenham's trial the jury considered it to be proved that she had bewitched a girl named Anne Thorn, aged sixteen, who, when sitting by the kitchen fire after having a dislocated knee set, was suddenly made to jump up and run half a mile, leap over a five-barred gate as nimble as a greyhound, gather some sticks and do them up in her gown and apron which she took off for the purpose, and run home again all in the space of six or seven minutes ; and to prove that Jane Wenham was undoubtedly a witch it was shown that though the bewitched girl flew at her and scratched her face with such "fury and eagerness that the noise of her nails seemed to all that were present as if she were scratching against a wainscot," yet no blood followed, also when Mr. Arthur Chauncy tried to draw blood from her by running a pin into her arm, "though

he ran it in frequently and left it in her arm so
that all the company might see it run up to the
head, yet she never winched for it, and there just
appeared a little thin watery serum, but nothing
that you can call blood," besides which she could
not say the Lord's Prayer properly, but made the
conclusive mistake of saying " Lead us not into
no temptation, but deliver us from all evil," while
to crown all, crooked pins appeared mysteriously,
and cats were seen about the place.   On this
overwhelming evidence, the jury found her guilty
of "conversing with the Devil in the shape of
a cat," and consequently Judge Powell had to
pronounce sentence of death on her, yet he seems
to have so far interested himself on her behalf
that she was ultimately reprieved, and placed by
Colonel Plummer of Gilston, in a small house
on his estate, in which she lived under his safe
protection for some years.   The public interest in
this trial was so great that at least seven different
pamphlets on the subject were published in 1712,
and one of them being written by the Rev.
Francis Bragge, vicar of Hitchin, one of the
witnesses against Jane Wenham, was so popular
that it ran into five editions or more, and four of
them were published within a month.

But perhaps, the Hertfordshire town best known in connection with witchcraft is Tring, which not only deserves mention as the residence of Isaac Tockfield, who in 1689 was bewitched with fits similar to those of the Baldwins of Sarratt, but it has also earned for itself the reputation of being the last place in Great Britain where witches were tested by "swimming," though the trial was actually made at the village of Long Marston, in Tring Parish. During the northern rebellion on behalf of the Pretender, Ruth Osborn, a poor old woman, asked John Butter-field, a dairyman, at Gubblecote, near Long Marston, for some butter-milk which he refused, saying, he had not enough for his hogs, where-upon she told him, that the Pretender would have him and his hogs too. Soon after several of his calves were ill, and when he removed to a public house he himself was attacked with fits, to which he had been subject in his youth. These misfortunes clearly proved that he was bewitched, and it was equally certain that Ruth Osborn had bewitched him, in revenge for the butter-milk affair of five years before, so on the advice of his neighbours he called in a wise woman from Northamptonshire, who not only confirmed the

15

witchcraft theory, but set a guard of six men
armed with staves and pitchforks, and themselves
protected by charms hung round their necks, to
watch him and his house night and day. However, this seem to have little or no effect. So
proclamation was made on market day, at
Winslow, Lughton Buzzard and Hemel Hampstead, to the following effect :—

> "This is to give notice that on Monday next, a man
> and woman are to be publicly ducked at Tring, for their
> crimes."

On the appointed day, April 22, 1757, Ruth
Osborn, and her husband John, sought sanctuary
in the church, but the "bigotted and superstitious
rioters," who had assembled in crowds from the
whole district round, not finding their victims,
smashed the workhouse windows and half
destroyed it, caught its governor, and threatened
to burn both him and the town, and searched the
whole premises, even to the "salt box," for the
reputed witches in vain. However, they were
found at last, dragged from the vestry, and their
thumbs and toes having been tied together they
were wrapped in sheets, and dragged by ropes
through a pond ; the woman was tried first, and
as she did not sink, Thomas Colley, a chimney

THE DUCKING OF JOHN OSBORN AND HIS WIFE, WRAPPED IN BLANKETS, ON A CHARGE OF WITCHCRAFT, NEAR TRING, IN HERTFORDSHIRE, BY WHICH THE WOMAN WAS DROWNED.

sweep, turned her over and over with a stick. John Osborn, the husband, was then tested in the same way, and the trial was made three times on each of them, with such success, that the woman died on the spot, and the man a few days later. When the experiment was over, Colley went round and collected money from the crowd for his trouble in shewing them such sport.

The coroner's verdict, however, declared that the Osborns had been murdered, and Colley was tried at Hertford Assizes, before Sir William Lee, and having been found guilty of murder, was sent back to the scene of the crime under the large escort of one hundred and eight men, seven officers, and two trumpeters, and was hung on August 24, 1751, at Gubblecote Cross, where his body swung in chains for many years.

Before his death he wrote a declaration recanting his belief in witchcraft, which was publicly read by the Vicar of Long Marston, but Clutterbuck writing in 1815, says that the belief in witchcraft was still strong in the neighbourhood, and some people seem inclined to assume that the laws of hereditary genius account for the presence of so many anti-vaccinators in the neighbourhood, at this day.

With the Tring episode, witchcraft in Herts seems to have ended, but in these days of spiritualism and its variants, it would be rash to assert that it will not break out afresh, and we therefore feel justified in giving a few well tried symptoms and remedies which might be found useful in case of any fresh outbreaks in the county ; these are taken from a medical work by William Drage, of Hitchin, published in 1668. "You may consider as bewitched those who vomit, with more or less torments, knives, scissors, eggs, dogs-tails, crooked nails, pins, needles, bits of wax, live eels, large pieces of flesh, stones, hooks, pieces of wood or saltpetre, or who fly, or run up the walls with their feet uppermost, or leap from one place to another strongly and fiercely at a great distance, also all who prophesy or speak in languages they never learned." For those so afflicted the best remedies to use are :—Coral, Rhue, Rosemary, Saint John's wort, Mistletoe, Ivy or Birch ;—probably the latter is best applied externally in the usual way—also quicksilver placed in a quill and laid under the pillow can do no harm ; against love charms a loadstone hung round the neck as an amulet is strongly recommended, though Mr. Drage is unable to mention cases in which anyone of these was entirely efficacious.

This account of withcraft in Hertfordshire is doubtless very imperfect, and there must exist records of many other cases, but the county historians have sadly neglected this important matter, and we can only hope that what little is here mentioned may induce some careful student of the past to write a complete history of all Hertfordshire witches.

Markets and Market Laws.

By W. R. WILLIS.

MARKETS in England date from a period anterior to the Norman Conquest. The market-stedes were of Anglo-Saxon origin, and point to the fact that although the old marks or communities raised their own food and clothing to a great extent, yet they were not entirely self-sufficing. With the growth of civilization new wants were created, which could not be locally supplied, while differences of soil, mineral wealth, and other circumstances led to the exchange of commodities between different communities. The need of salt for preserving meat had much to do with the creation of markets. This valuable article could not be universally procured; hence it had to be conveyed to centres, where it was exchanged for goods common to that district, and the place where these exchanges or barters were effected came to be called markets. They were originally on the boundary between the two "marks," and the spot was often indicated by a stone, the precursor of the "market-cross" of mediæval times. So far as the writer is aware, there is no extant example of a market stone in Hertfordshire, but there is a fine instance in the "four shires' stone," at Moreton-in-Marsh, which is situated at the junction of the four counties of Gloucester, Hereford, Worcester, and Warwick. Lack of means of communication with the larger centres of populations, and the manufacturing towns, favoured the growth of markets or fairs, for the two events were originally one. The markets at first took place only at stated intervals during the year ; shrines and burial-places of noted men were the most frequented spots for the annual fairs. A fair once or twice or even thrice a year was not sufficient to meet the requirements of the case, and so in course of time the fair became a distinct institution from the market, the latter being held weekly, and the former generally once a year, usually on the feast-day, or festival of the patronal saint of the parish.

The right to establish a market was jealously guarded. In the majority of cases, they were established by Royal Charter in the boroughs, while in the smaller towns, the Lords of the Manor granted leave to form a market, and

exacted tolls on all the animals or goods sold
therein.   In Abbey towns the Abbots were
usually the owners of the market, made laws for
its regulation, and took the tolls ; they were
generally, it may be remarked in passing, the
Lords of the Manor in which the Abbey was
situated.

At Hertford, the two markets, on Thursdays
and Saturdays, were conferred on the town by
Charter of Edward III. ; and in the reign of
Queen Mary a further Charter of Incorporation
was granted to the burgesses and tenants of Hertford, confirming to them and their successors these
markets, and ordering that no markets should be
held on either of those days within seven miles of
the town.   As showing the exclusive character of
the times, a declaration was added "that if any
corn or merchandise was sold in Ware, or elsewhere, within seven miles of the town, the same
might be seized and forfeited by the bailiffs and
porters of Hertford."   The fair was established at
a later date.   On the marriage of the ill-fated
Henry VI. with Margaret of Anjou, the Castle
and Honor of Hertford formed part of her settle-
ment.   In a Charter afterwards executed by her,
she gave liberty to the bailiff and constable of the

Borough to hold "a horse fair in such part of the town as they should deem expedient."

Some of the markets were established by Charter, others by prescription. That at St. Albans seems to have partaken of a dual character. It was originally included in the charter which Richard I. gave to the Abbot of St. Albans. The Burgesses afterwards obtained a Charter from the Abbot, which they subsequently surrendered. The earliest Charter of Incorporation possessed by the borough is that of Edward VI., which confirms the market, and also directs that the Mayor shall be Clerk of the Market. The same Charter established a Court Leet which took cognizance of petty offences.

The duties of a Court Leet in a manor appear to have been discharged by the Common Council. Offenders against the market laws, comprised within the constitution, were presented to the Court by several officials to whom was entrusted the task of seeing that the regulations were obeyed. Thus, "the Mayor, as Clerk of the Market, had the power of fixing the price of bread, beer, ale, wine, and all other victuals sold in the borough. Flesh and fish tasters were appointed, whose duty it was to see that no corrupt flesh or fish was sold. . . . . The Viewers of the Market of the Cross had to see that all food offered for sale there was wholesome, and to properly regulate the market." Our ancestors were not only very particular as to how, when and where commodities should be sold, but they endeavoured to promote honesty of trading by fixing in the Assize of Bread both the quality and the price of the article. Three hundred years ago, complaints were rife that the bakers gave short weight and used ingredients of inferior quality. Throughout the country, the records of the Courts Leet contain entries recording convictions against offenders in this particular. One entry from the Corporation Minute Books of St. Albans will suffice.

At the Court held November 24th, 1595, it is recorded :—

> "William Pharoe, for that his 2d. wheaten loaf did want seven ounces, besides other defaults, 3s. 4d."

This Pharoe appears to have been incorrigible, for, together with several fellow-townsmen, he was fined at the next Court for a very similar offence.

"King Henry II. fixed upon Berkhamsted as a favourite place of residence. He constantly kept his court here, and gave a substantial

proof of the esteem in which he held our town by
granting to us our first regular charter.   In this
charter, which was given at Oxford, on the 1st
June, A.D. 1156, in the presence of Theobald,
Archbishop of Canterbury, after the assertion that
the men and merchants of Berkhamsted and
Wallingford which is coupled with it, are to enjoy
their priviledges as well and as honorably, and
better and more honorably, than in the days of
King Edward, King William, and King Henry,
we find a declaration that they are to be free of
all tolls and duties whithersoever they go, whether
through England, Normandy, or Spain ; and any
one disquieting them is to forfeit £10.   It may be
well to remark here that there is an instance of
the assertion of this privilege in the Black
Prince's time, when the Bailiff of Aylesbury's
goods were distrained at Berkhamsted, for having
taken toll of the tenants of this manor.   This
portion too of the grant is again recited and
confirmed in the second year of King Richard
III., by John Rector of Ashridge."

The foregoing account of Berkhamsted Market,
from Cobb's " History of Berkhamsted," may be
supplemented by the fact that at the beginning
of the reign of Henry III. the market day at

Berkhamsted was changed from Sunday to Monday, on May 7th, 1217.

A Court of Pie Poudre, or Dusty Feet, corresponded in its duties in this respect to the common council, and such a court was held at Hemel Hempstead, which took count of petty offences in the market and the fair. This Court still discharges some of its old functions, being presided over by the High Bailiff. It was usual after the business of the Court of Dusty Feet had been concluded for the High Bailiff and the attendants of the Court to go over the Bailiwick property, and in company with the Recorder and Under Bailiff to inspect the stalls in the market. A Court of Pie Poudre was also held at Hertford, and the Bailiffs were entrusted with the collection of the impost "stalpans" or stallage, a payment made for the liberty of pitching goods or erecting stalls and booths either in the fair or the market. Our forefathers were not well inclined to strangers, and the ferocious laws against vagabonds have their counterparts in the stringent regulations respecting strangers in general, and especially in the markets. The exclusive spirit of the old traders is exhibited in some of the market laws at St. Albans, where every butcher who sold meat

within the borough "was compelled to bring in
weekly the hides and tallow, under a penalty of
five shillings for each offence.   Outsiders were
not allowed to sell their wares in the town except
on fair days."

It may be noted *en passant* that Lincoln
Corporation enacted that "no stranger or trades-
man not being free of this city to set up any stall
or sell any wares on Market Days."   The Court
Leet records at Selby, in Yorkshire, for the
sixteenth century, contain a typical entry :—
"Decreed 30s. against John Wilkinson for
buying of corn being no inhabiter within this
liberty contrary to the statute in that case
provided and against the order of this town."

The conduct of the market was regulated by
numerous local enactments.   One provided that
no higlers should buy or sell any goods in the
market until a bell had rung.   This bell was
regularly rung at St. Albans at nine o'clock in the
morning by the town crier, and the practice has
survived till the present day.   It was the duty of
the Bailiffs of the borough to see to the ringing
of the market bell, to the keeping clean of the
market-place, and also to attend the markets and
fairs,

In order that the dignity and importance of the local authorities might be maintained, and the ancient privileges of freemen duly recognised, the Common Council of St. Albans enacted that what time the worthy mayor sat as Clerk of the Market, to receive the report of the viewers, and to hear complaints, he should wear his municipal robes, on penalty of a fine for default.

Tolls in the market were also a valuable asset of the manor or of the borough where the burgesses owned the market. So valuable were they in some instances that a good round sum had to be paid as compensation to the proprietor, when the town desired to acquire the market. At Watford, the Earl of Essex owned the market as Lord of the Manor, and exacted tolls on all cattle and sheep and other animals which were sold therein. A proposal to remove the cattle market from the main thoroughfare of the town to a more convenient locality had to be abandoned some years ago on account of the great cost involved in acquiring the market rights from the Lord of the Manor. In a few instances the burgesses were entitled to the tolls on payment of a yearly rent. Thus at Hertford, where three yearly fairs were held under the Charter of Queen Mary, the burgesses were empowered " to receive stallage, piceage, and all other profits, amerciaments, actions, commodities, and emoluments whatsoever, with all liberties and free customs pertaining to such fairs, paying 13s. 4d. to the Queen for the three fairs, at Michaelmas every year."

At St. Albans the right to levy tolls belonged to the Corporation, and in 1699 " persons selling grain and other things in the markets and fairs, without paying toll, were ordered to be prosecuted." Yet the right to levy fees on all corn sold was not acquiesced in by the farmers, and at the Court of Common Council in 1795, " the lessee of the tolls complained that persons brought samples of corn to market and not the whole quantity, and refused to pay toll for more than was actually brought into the Market House, whereby he was much injured in the receipt of tolls. Resolved, that the toll was due on all corn sold on Market Day, whether into the Market House, or not." The corporation here leased the tolls ; in 1828 they realised £150. At that meeting, the council decided to prohibit the sale of corn by sample, and to enforce the sale by bulk. The tolls were applied to public purposes in the Abbey Town. They were not always

16

devoted to that end, for a writ of Richard I. to
the Barons of the Exchequer, ordered them "also
to pay 25s. to the church, from the market of
Lichfield, for the soul of Henry II., to be specially
mentioned by the said church."

Where the tolls were held by a private owner,
as at Ware, they were much esteemed.   "Thomas
Fanshaw, purchaser of the Manor of Ware upon
a *quo warranto* brought against him in Hilary
Term, anno 27 Elizabeth claimed to have one
market on Tuesday in every week within the
town of Ware by prescription (*i.e.* by its having
been handed down to him among the rights and
privileges of his manor), with a Court of Pie
Poudre and view of Frank Pledge and all the
tenants and residents, assizes, and assay of bread,
wine, and ale, and other victuals," all of which
liberties and privileges were allowed and adjudged
to him upon the said *quo warranto.*

Among the most important laws regulating
markets were those which related to fore-stalling,
or engrossing, which may be traced back to the
days of Edward III.   In 1350 a statute was
passed, rendering anyone buying articles of food
on the way to a market liable to forfeit the
things bought, or to two years' imprisonment.

The occasion for the law was that various traders
attempted to intercept the commodities with a
view to obtaining a monopoly and thus raising the
price.   Sometimes they endeavoured to increase
the price.   Subsequent Acts of Parliament were
passed with a view to suppressing forestalling,
engrossing and regrating, and it was only in July,
1844, that they were finally repealed.   Moreover,
many manorial and market rules which had their
origin in the laws against forestalling are retained
to the present.

An ancient usage connected with markets,
references to which are frequently met with in the
literature of the period, was the expenditure of the
" market penny" or money for liquor on the market
day.   Thus in " Poor Robin " (1735) we have :—

" Crispin falls very lucky this year, for being on
a Saturday, they can go to market, buy victuals,
and spend the market penny in a morning, dine at
noon, drink and enjoy themselves all the afternoon, and they that are sober husbands may go to
bed at a proper hour nevertheless."

For the extracts from the archives of the St.
Albans Court of Common Council, I am indebted
to Mr. A. E. Gibbs' excellent transcription of the
" Corporation Records of St. Albans."

The Great Bed of Ware.

EVERYONE, it may be presumed, has heard something about the Great Bed of Ware, the fame of which has been built up, in a great measure, on casual allusions to it in the dramatic literature of a past age. The earliest of these occurs in Shakespeare's play of "Twelfth Night," in the second scene of the third act of which *Sir Toby Belch* says, in reference to the challenge of *Sir Andrew Aguecheek*, "Go, write it in a martial hand; be curst and brief; it is no matter how witty, so it be eloquent, and full of invention: taunt him with the license of ink; if thou *thou*'st him some thrice, it shall not be amiss; and as many lies as will lie in thy sheet of paper, although the sheet were big enough for the Bed of Ware." In a much later comedy, Farquhar's "Recruiting Officer," *Sergeant Kite* speaks of the bed of honour as "a mighty large bed, bigger by half than the Great Bed of Ware. Ten thousand people may be in it together, and never feel one another."

Though the celebrity of the bed, or rather bedstead, in former times, may be inferred from these
allusions, there is very little to be gathered concerning it from the county historians. Clutterbuck's
account of it is as follows :—" One of the inns at
Ware, known by the name of the Saracen's Head,
contains a bed of unusually large dimensions,
measuring twelve feet square, consisting wholly
of oak, curiously and elaborately carved. After
diligent inquiry, I have not been able to meet
with any written document, or local tradition,
which throws any light upon the history of this
curious bed, to which allusion is made by Shakespeare, in his play of 'Twelfth Night.' There is
a date of 1463 painted on the back of the bed ;
but it appears to be more modern than the bed
itself, which, from the style of the carving, may be
referred to the age of Queen Elizabeth." Chauncy
adds to this account a statement of the bed having
at one time received twelve men and their wives,
who laid six of each sex at the top and six at the
bottom, which would allow only one foot to each
person, the bed being twelve feet square, the
mode of arrangement being, first, a man, then two
women, and so on, two men and two women
alternately, with the sixth man on the outside, like

the first. This arrangement differs from that given by Chauncy ; but it is the only one which will support his statement that no man was near to any woman other than his wife.

The story commonly told concerning this remarkable bedstead is, that it was made by one Jonas Fosbrooke, a journeyman carpenter, and presented by him to Edward IV., in 1463, as a rare specimen of wood carving, and for the use of the royal family, or for the accommodation of princes and nobles on any great occasion. The king is said to have been much pleased with the workmanship and the great industry of the maker, and to have rewarded him with a pension for life. This story, or the tradition which gives the possession of this unique article of furniture to the Earl of Warwick of that period, may be taken to explain the date of 1463 on the back of the bedstead, though it was probably painted at a later period as an apparent confirm-ation of the story. The cumbrous couch is said to have subsequently been sold, amongst other furniture belonging to Warwick, at Ware Park.

There was a ghostly legend attached to the bed at a later date, according to which, after being unused for many years by any royal or noble

THE GREAT BED OF WARE.

persons, it was appropriated to any large parties
when the town was very full of strangers, as
on such occasions as hunting parties, notable
weddings, etc. It was said that, whenever it
was so used, the occupants were unable to sleep,
being disturbed throughout the night by un-
accountable pinchings and scratchings, so that
after some time no one would sleep in it. The
cause of this nocturnal trouble was supposed to be
that the spirit of Jonas Fosbrooke hovered about
his favourite piece of workmanship, and being
vexed at its being used for the accommodation of
persons of inferior degree, intended as it had been
for only princes and nobles to rest upon, strove to
prevent such low-born persons from obtaining any
sleep beneath its broad canopy.

There was also a story told of one Harrison
Saxby, master of the horse to Henry VIII., who,
having fallen in love with the daughter of a miller
and maltster residing at Chalk Island, near Ware,
and knowing that she had other suitors of her
own social standing, swore that he would do
anything to win her. This coming to the ears of
the King as he was passing through Ware, on his
way to Hertford, he caused the girl and all her
suitors to be brought before him, and, in the

arrogant and dominating manner which the
Tudors possessed in a pre-eminent degree,
promised her hand to him who would sleep one
night in the Great Bed, provided he were found
there in the morning. The rustic suitors were all
deterred by superstitious fears from accepting this
test of the ardour of their passion, but Saxby
expressed his willingness to stand the ordeal, and
retired to the chamber which his rivals shrank
from entering. The result strengthened the ill
odour to which the famous bed had come ; for, on
the following morning, when the King's attendants
entered the room, the master of the horse was
found on the floor, covered with bruises, and in
a state of exhaustion. So, at least, runs the story.

The Great Bed is said to have been kept in
former times at the Old Crown Inn, to which, if
there is any truth in the tradition which attributes
its possession to the Earl of Warwick, it must be
supposed to have been removed from Ware Park
on the occasion of the sale of the King-maker's
effects. It seems, as in later times, to have been
made a show of, on which occasions the ceremony
of drinking a mug of ale to some toast was
performed. There appears to be no record of
its removal to the Saracen's Head, where it

remained for many years subsequent to the time
when it was seen by Clutterbuck. It was there
offered for sale by auction in September, 1864,
when it was put up at a hundred guineas, at
which price, there being no advance upon it, it
was bought in.

The present resting-place of this unique piece
of furniture is the Rye House Inn, an old timber
and plaster building, between Broxbourne and
Hoddesdon. The inn takes its name from a
ruinous red brick building on the opposite side
of the road, part of a castle dating from the
middle of the fifteenth century, which in the
seventeenth became the locality of a plot for
the assassination of Charles II. and his brother.
Many circumstances combine to make the inn a
popular place of resort during the summer. In
addition to its historical associations, many persons
supposing it to be the identical scene of the Rye
House plot, there is a museum of local antiquities
and curiosities, including the Great Bed, in connection with it, while its contiguity to both the
river Lea and the Great Eastern Railway, renders
it a favourite resort of anglers.

The Death and Resting-place of the Great Lord Bacon.

By John T. Page.

> "The great deliverer he! who from the gloom
> Of cloister'd monks, and jargon-teaching schools,
> Led forth the true Philosophy, there long
> Held in the magic chain of words and forms."

IN his famous essay on Bacon, Lord Macaulay tells us that "from the day of his death his fame has been constantly and steadily progressive." To the "next age" Bacon bequeathed his name and memory. This shows how well he judged the lasting value of his work. He knew instinctively that it was based on a firm foundation, and that if his life and work could only be separated and assayed apart on their respective merits, the latter would undoubtedly come out of the crucible pure and sterling in its worth. The wording of his will shows that he deemed many episodes of his life to have been animated by base and sordid motives; it also betrays a genuine confidence as to the quality of his legacy to the world at large.

It is passing strange that two of the greatest

minds the world has ever seen, those of Bacon
and Shakespeare, should have existed contempor-
aneously.   Neither before nor since their time
have such prodigies of intellect appeared.   Dean
Church, in speaking of the two, aptly terms
Bacon's "the highest, richest, largest mind but
one, in the age which had seen Shakespeare
and his fellows."   Alluding to the controversy
which has raged (and possibly may be still raging)
around these two great names, he adds that
Bacon's mind was "so bright and rich and large
that there have even been found those who identify
him with the writer of *Hamlet* and *Othello*.   That
is idle.   Bacon could no more have written the
plays than Shakespeare could have prophecied
the triumphs of natural philosophy."   This criticism
is just, and shows at a glance the characteristics
and limits of these two great minds.

It is not the intention of the writer to even
briefly pass in review the chief events in the life
of the great Lord Bacon.   Suffice it to say that
although he must have spent much of his time in
Hertfordshire, especially in his latter days, he was
not a native of the county.   His father's (Sir
Nicholas Bacon, Queen Elizabeth's Lord Keeper)
country mansion was at Gorhambury, hard by St.

Albans, and his town residence York House, in the Strand. Francis Bacon was born at the latter place on the 22nd of January, 1560-61. His brilliant parts easily secured for him the highest honours, and the story of his illustrious career and untimely fall presents one of the most pathetic object-lessons in the annals of English history. "With all its glories, it was the greatest ship-wreck, the greatest tragedy of an age which saw many."*

The opening days of the year 1621 saw the great Lord Chancellor Bacon, Baron Verulam, created Viscount St. Albans, and in the early days of May of the same year we find him convicted of bribery and corruption, heavily fined, and for a short time actually committed to prison. He survived his disgrace for the space of five years, during which time he devoted his energies to a revision of his works and the study of experimental philosophy. His town residence, York House, had gone to pay his debts, and the only place in London he could really call home was the lodging of his lawyer-days in Gray's Inn. Here, at Gorhambury and at a friend's house in Fulham, he seems to have divided his time. He never

* Church.

ceased to bewail his misfortunes, and several times
made efforts to regain the position he had lost ;
but at the same time his mind was continuously
active in his endeavours to solve the problems of
natural law.   Never was a chance let slip of
adding to his stock of practical knowledge and his
methods were characteristically exemplified in the
last experiment he ever made.   This is best told
in the words of Aubrey, the following account
being taken from his MSS. now deposited in the
Ashmolean Museum at Oxford :—

"The cause of his lordship's death was trying
an experiment as he was taking the aire in the
coach with Dr. Witherborne, a Scotchman,
physitian to the king, towards Highgate : snow lay
upon the ground, and it came into my lord's
thoughts, why flesh might not be preserved in
snow, as in salt.   They were resolved they would
try the experiment presently.   They alighted out
of the coach, and went into a poor woman's house
at the bottome of Highgate-hill, and bought a hen,
and made the woman exenterate it, and then
stuffed the body with snow ; and my lord did help
to do it himself.   The snow so chilled him he
immediately fell so ill, that he could not return to
his lodgings (I suppose then at Gray's Inn), but

went to the Earl of Arundell's house * at Highgate, where they put him into a good bed, warmed
with a panne ; but it was a damp bed that had
not been lain in for about a yeare before, which
gave him such a cold, that in two or three days
. . . he died of suffocation."

An aged friend, Sir Julius Cæsar, Master of the
Rolls, watched assiduously by the bedside of
Bacon through the fleeting hours of his fatal illness
and to him he dictated his last letter. It was
addressed to the Earl of Arundel, the owner of
the house whose hospitable doors had opened to
receive him in his extremity, and certainly does
not convey the idea that he imagined his end was
near. The probability is that ere the letter had
reached its destination the ex-lord-chancellor was
no more. Fortunately the document has been
preservéd, and from it we are able to gather some
of the last thoughts which occupied the mind of
the great philosopher. Writing to "my very
good lord," he says :—

"I was likely to have had the fortune of Caius
Plinius the elder, who lost his life by trying an
experiment about the burning of the mountain

---

* Arundel House stood upon the slope of Highgate Hill. Its exact site
is now matter of conjecture. It was pulled down in 1825.

Vesuvius. For I was also desirous to try an experiment or two touching the conservation and induration of bodies. As for the experiment itself, it succeeded exceedingly well; but in the journey between London and Highgate, I was taken with such a fit of casting, as I know not whether it was the stone, or some surfeit, or cold, or, indeed, a touch of them all three.

"But when I came to your lordship's house I was not able to go back, and therefore was forced to take up my lodgings here, where your housekeeper is very careful and diligent about me; which I assure myself your lordship will not only pardon towards him, but think the better of him for it. For indeed your lordship's house was happy to me; and I kiss your noble hands, for the welcome which I am sure you give me to it. I know how unfit it is for me to write to your lordship with any other hands than my own; but, by my troth, my fingers are so disjoynted with this fit of sickness, that I cannot steadily hold a pen."

Bacon's death occurred in the early morning of Easter day, the 9th of April, 1626.* His will

---

* Hepworth Dixon (Personal History of Lord Bacon from unpublished papers) gives the date of his death as the 1st of November, 1625.

17

contained the following clause :—" For my burial I desire it may be in St. Michael's Church, St. Albans ; there was my mother buried, and it is the parish church of my mansion house of Gorhambury, and it is the only Christian church within the walls of ancient Verulam." Sir Thomas Meautys, Bacon's cousin, private secretary and faithful friend, inherited his family possessions, and he it was who carried out his " master's " obsequies. The funeral was not in any sense of a public character, and but few details are recorded concerning it. The remains were removed from Highgate to Gorhambury, and then, in accordance with the directions contained in the will, were quietly and unostentatiously interred in the chancel of St. Michael's Church.*

Bacon's monument is unique in design and execution, and once seen is never to be forgotten. It occupies a niche in the wall on the north side of the chancel, and consists of a white marble statue within an arched recess, and below it a Latin inscription. The figure of the philosopher is represented as seated in a high-backed chair, wearing a broad-brimmed hat, and dressed in a

---

* The body of Sir Thomas Meautys was eventually laid to rest at Bacon's feet. The inscription on the stone which covers his remains has now unfortunately become obliterated,

chancellor's gown, trunk hose and large circular
ruff. The right hand hangs carelessly over the
arm of the chair, and the left elbow leans upon the
chair arm and thence supports the head. The
shoes are ornamented with large rosettes, and
bands with long ends are tied round the knees.
The attitude of the figure is one of reposeful
contemplation, but to some the wearing of the hat
seems to suggest an appearance of irreverence.
The epitaph was written by Sir Henry Wotton,
and is inscribed in three separate compartments,
below the alcove containing the statue :—

FRANCISCVS BACON BARO DE VERVLĀ Sᴛᴀ ALBᴺᴵ VICᴹˢ

SEV NOTORIBVS TITVLIS

SCIENTIARVM LVMEN FACVNDIÆ LEX

SIC SEDEBAT.

———

QVI POSTQVAM OMNIA NATVRALIS SAPIENTIÆ

ET CIVILIS ARCANA EVOLVISSET

NATVRÆ DECRETVM EXPLEVIT

COMPOSITA SOLVANTVR

Anᵒ Dɴɪ MDCXXVI

ÆTAT LXVI.

———

TANTA VIRI

MEM.

THOMAS MEAVTYS

SVPERSTITIS CVLTOR

DEFVNCTO ADMIRATOR

H. P.

———

(Translation.)
Francis Bacon
Baron of Verulam, Viscount St. Albans
or, by more conspicuous titles
of Science the Light, of Eloquence the Law,
sat thus.

———

Who after all Natural Wisdom
And Secrets of Civil Life he had unfolded,
Nature's Law fulfilled—
Let Compounds be Dissolved!
in the year of our Lord 1626, aged 66.

———

Of such a man, that the Memory might remain
Thomas Meautys
living his Attendant, dead his Admirer
placed this Monument.

The sculptor of the monument is unknown, but
it is an interesting fact that it has attracted attention
as a work of art quite as much as for the sake of
its subject.   A full sized replica of the original has
been electrotyped, and occupies a conspicuous
position in the National Portrait Gallery, in
London.

The Romance of the Road.

By W. R. Willis.

"WHERE," asks Thackeray in "Vanity Fair," "is the road now, and its merry incidents of life? Is there no Chelsea or Greenwich for the old honest, pimple-nosed coachmen? I wonder where they are, those good fellows. Is old Welsh alive or dead? And the waiters; yea, and the inns at which they waited, and the cold rounds of beef inside, and the stunted ostler with his blue nose and clinking pail; where is he, and where is his generation?"

So far as the county of Hertford is concerned, he has disappeared for ever, although attempts have been made by the periodical running of coaches to Hertford and St. Albans to revive in some degree the ancient glory of the road, and to rehabilitate a few of its picturesque incidents.

The contiguity of Hertfordshire to the metropolis has from the earliest times given an importance to the highways which traverse it, and the county is blessed with more trunk roads crossing its length than falls to the lot of most shires of its somewhat small area. In the matter of the roads, Hertford-

262 of 308

shire dates back to the Roman occupation, when
well‑constructed military thoroughfares from
London and the ancient city of Verulam wound
their way north and south. The courses of these
highways have been somewhat diverted, but in
the main they follow their original directions.

The Hertfordshire roads in the mediæval times
presented many a scene of picturesque activity.
Gay cavalcades, on warlike errand or on pleasure
bent, have moved along them, which in common
with the rest of the country, presented all the
disagreeable features, so far as the unevenness of
the surface was concerned, that distinguished the
highways of the ante‑turnpike days. Considera‑
tions of space preclude one from detailing the
martial processions which issued from feudal castle
or manorial hall, or the troops which hurried to
meet each other in the fatal struggles at St. Albans
and Gladsmuir Heath (Barnet) in the Wars of the
Roses, or of the marchings and counter marchings
of the Royalist and Parliamentary hosts, in their
ten years' contest. The part which Hertfordshire
and its roads then played belongs to the history of
the country.

Ecclesiastical pageants were not uncommon in
mediæval Hertfordshire, and the great ecclesiastics

and their retinue from St. Albans, whether attend-
ing the Lord Abbot on his journey to Parliament,
or accompanying some of the monastic officers on
a visitation to a subordinate cell or priory, would
be a frequent spectacle. The old priory at Friern
Barnet, in Middlesex, known to the present inhabitants of the district as the Friary, was the
scene of many of these visits. The journey thither
must have been accomplished with difficulty, for
the way led along the ancient road from South
Mimms to the back of Wrotham Park, and thence
through Hadley to Whetstone. In many places
it was a perfect quagmire, and at the best of times
and in the finest weather the inequalities of surface
would render a journey on horseback or on foot
a most unpleasant experience.

Contemporary records have preserved to us an
account of some of these processions. Mr. F. E.
Baines * thus pictures the scene :—" On March
22nd, 1426, the monks of St. Alban's Abbey
marched in solemn procession to Barnet. The
peck of March dust, which blew from the east
over Gladsmuir Heath and the open ground where
Hadley Church now stands, plentifully besprinkled
the cavalcade, yet it was a splendid sight for the

* " On Track of the Mail Coach."

villagers. At the head of the column rode the Duke of Gloucester ; after him, his retinue ; at his right side, perhaps princes of the Church ; at his bridle hand, the secular power. Behind came the monks chanting a service as they approached the dwellings of men, the trappings of the horses and the lance heads of the spearmen flashing back the rays of the westering sun as it sank over the wooded ridge of Dyrham Park and Elstree Vale."

The wretched state of the roads in the pre-Macadamite days of 1656 is clearly indicated in a petition to the Quarter Sessions for relief sent up by the inhabitants of Radwell setting out that they had always done their best to maintain the highways in the parish, yet, despite their care, " their said highways stand in much need of repair, which they are no ways able to perform (though the whole revenue of the parish should be employed) the Great North Road lying for two miles together in the said parish, and the nature of the soil being such as the winter devours whatsoever they are able to lay on in the summer and the parish is so small that it hath in it all but two teams."

A graphic description of the discomforts and dangers of country travelling about the beginning of the eighteenth century in the county of Hertford is given by Thoresby, who tells us in his diary how the rains had "raised the washes upon the road near Ware to the height that passengers from London that were upon the road swam, and a poor higgler was drowned, which prevented me travelling for many hours ; yet toward evening we adventured with some country people who conducted us over the meadows, whereby we missed the deepest of the wash at Cheshunt, though we rode to the saddle-skirts for a considerable way, but got safe to Waltham Cross."

The pack horses were succeeded by huge lumbering stage waggons, which required four and oftentimes more horses to propel them, and even then were unable to negotiate the softer roads.   Such havoc did their great wheels and heavy loads work upon the highways that they were frequently forbidden by resolutions of the Court Leet to enter a town in rainy weather. Fortunately, bad as were many of the roads in Herts, they were immeasurably superior to those in some other parts of the country, even so recently as the beginning of the century.   At Lyme Regis, for instance, a little more than a hundred years ago, no vehicles were kept at all, and all the carrying was done by pack-horses.

But the perils arising from the badness of the roads were not the only danger to which travellers by the stage waggon were exposed. In the year 1700 we learn that the London stage waggon, belonging to Mr. Truman of Derby, travelled along the North Road through Barnet, Hatfield, Welwyn, and Hitchin, and when it had got beyond the latter town and was approaching Biggleswade the candle of the lantern caught the tilt of the waggon, and set fire to it. The flames spread rapidly, and consumed the contents of the waggon, igniting a cask of spirituous liquors, which exploded.

Personal dangers also attended the travellers. In 1786 a young woman journeyed to St. Albans by the stage waggon, was watched to leave it by a soldier, who then murdered her.

With the year 1755 came the passing of the Turnpike Act, and an appreciable improvement in the roads. Singularly enough, the change in the roads was not appreciated by the class who chiefly benefited by it, and it is related of more than one waggoner that he refused to use the new roads, preferring to journey along the old thoroughfares with all their risks and discomforts. In fact one conservative member of the class declared that he "required but a five-feet width in a lane, and all the rest might go to the devil."   But before the adoption of the Turnpike Act stage-coaches had begun to replace the lumbering waggons, and they frequently performed the journey at the then phenomenal speed of eight to ten miles an hour. One of the earliest regular coaches put upon the Hertfordshire roads was that which ran from London to Hitchin and Bedford, and continued to be run by John Shrimpton (the originator) and his descendants until the advent of the railway terminated its career.   The following is a copy of the advertisement announcing the new departure :

"HITCHIN AND BEDFORD.

Stage coaching in one day ! Sets out from the Greyhound Inn in Smithfield, London, every Tuesday, Thursday, and Saturday to the Sun Inn at Hitchin, and returns to for London every Monday, Wednesday, and Friday.   Also goes every Tuesday morning AT THREE OF THE CLOCK precisely, from the Greyhound inn afore said, to the Swan Inn, Bedford, and returns every Wednesday from London and goes through Hatfield, Welling, Stevenage, Hitchin, Alicey, Hendlow, Southill, Old Warden, and Coalington to Bedford.

Performed (if God permit)
by
JOHN SHRIMPTON.

The stage begins on Tuesday, the 23rd March, 1741-2, for Hitchin ; and on Tuesday, the 13th of April for Bedford."

The two main roads to the north and north-west, the Great North Road which went through Barnet, Hatfield, and Hitchin for York, and the north-western road which united at St. Albans the old Edgware road and the new road which Telford had cut through South Mimms from Barnet to the Abbey town, were thronged with coaches at the latter end of the eighteenth and the beginning of the present century. The eastern road through Cheshunt and Bishop Stortford, was also well patronised, being the most direct route from London to Cambridge, and having also branches to East Anglia. With the advent of Mr. Palmer's mail coaches, in 1785, the activity of the roads was greatly increased, and the breeding of horses received a considerable stimulus. The mail coaches for York, Newcastle, Leeds, Scotland, Carlisle, Liverpool, Kendal, Manchester, and Holyhead, not to enumerate others, passed along the Hertfordshire roads, as well as the mails intended for Cambridge. When Telford's great engineering feat built a new Barnet Hill, and thus obviated the terrible pull up the old hill to the church, a portion of which road is still extant to the left of the hill as the traveller enters Barnet from London, he considerably lightened the task of horses and drivers alike.　His new road from near the Green Dragon, in Hadley High Street, to South Mimms, and thus to St. Albans, was the means of diverting many of the mail coaches from the North Road to the Holyhead Road.　Mr. Baines records that the first mail coach to pass through St. Albans was the Liverpool mail which left the Mersey town on July 25th, 1785 ; "the very first, in fact, of Palmer's mails to run over the Great North Road."

Foot passengers and solitary riders were much exposed to the menaces and attacks of highwaymen.　A favourite resort of Dick Turpin was Brownswells, a portion of the North Road, just over the Middlesex border, and opposite the extensive cemetery of the Islington Burial Board. From this rendezvous the notorious ruffian frequently penetrated into the adjacent county, and the neighbourhood of Barnet, Potters Bar, and Mimms are full of traditions of this particular highwayman.　The celebrated ride to York from London in one day, erroneously attributed to Turpin, took place along the North Road, from Whetstone to Hitchin.　This remarkable feat, by which a distance of 197 miles was covered by one mount, was really achieved some sixty years

before Turpin's day by William Nevison, the
renowned Yorkshire highwayman, or "road
inspector" as he was sometimes euphemistically
termed.

The hero of "Rookwood," however, had
many associations with the county, and once
very narrowly escaped apprehension at Hertford.
After the murder of an assistant ranger of Epping
Forest, Turpin found it convenient to retire from
the neighbourhood. He went in search of his
colleague, Tom King, and sent word for his wife
to meet him at a certain public-house at Hertford.
With two friends she repaired to the hostelry, and
there awaited the arrival of her spouse. Turpin
came up shortly after, and enquired for her under
an assumed name. Ascertaining she was there,
he was about to make his way to join her in the
kitchen when he was accosted by a butcher, to
whom he was indebted to the amount of £5.
The butcher requested repayment of the money,
as "it would be of great service." Turpin replied
that he had no money upon him, but that his wife
was in the house, and he would get it from her.
The unsuspecting butcher rejoined his companions,
and communicated to them the name of the visitor,
informing them that he intended first to recover

his money, and then seize Turpin, for whose arrest a substantial reward was offered. Instead of going to his wife, Turpin immediately got through a window into the yard, mounted his horse, and galloped away, leaving the expectant butcher to make the unpleasant discovery that his bird had flown.

The troublesomeness of these predatory denizens of the roads at the latter end of the seventeenth century is proved by a writ (dated October 21, 1697) from the chief constable to the constable of St. Andrew's Hertford, "that whereas it is manifest that the roads are so infested with robbers that it is highly dangerous for persons to travel with any sum of money, he is to provide five or six able-bodied men, without horses, and cause them to be well armed with muskets, carbines or guns well loaded and fit for execution, and cause them to be ready in the market place at Hertford to-morrow morning at half-past six."

Anent the attacks on wayfarers by footpads, Mr. Stevens relates in his "Old Barnet" a very good story. A traveller was walking from St. Albans to Barnet when he was attacked by a ruffianly cutpurse. Being a bold, strong man, he proved the better of his antagonist, and as he was also armed with a pistol, he was able to turn the tables. He bade his assailant, on threat of being immediately shot if he desisted, to walk before him into Barnet up to the cage which stood near Wood Street. Arrived there, he went to fetch the keys, "prudently telling his prisoner to wait outside," and, naturally enough, when he returned he found he was well rid of a troublesome rogue. It was a time when anyone venturing far from the precincts of a town needed to be well protected. The provision made by a Dorsetshire man for a young relative about to undertake a long journey was most acceptable. "John," he said, "I've cut a good blackthorn, that'll stand your friend."

These desperadoes of the road attacked the mails oftentimes with impunity. The following notice, issued by the Postmaster General, records a daring robbery on 1st March, 1810, of Hertfordshire mails at Barnet :—

"Whereas the bags of letters from this office (London) of last night, for the the following towns, viz. :—

Hatfield,
Welwyn,
Stevenage,
Baldock.
Biggleswade, [other towns are also set out].

were stolen from the mail-box, about ten o'clock on the

same night, supposed at Barnet, by forcibly wrenching off the lock whilst the horses were changing ; whoever shall apprehend and convict, or cause to be apprehended and convicted, the person or persons who stole the said bags, shall be entitled to a reward of One Hundred Pounds."

The perpetrators of these outrages occasionally had recourse to most desperate means to facilitate the robberies ; at least it is difficult to imagine that an incident of the following kind could have been dictated by any other motive than that of robbery. On the night of June 5th, 1805, a gate was placed in the middle of the turnpike road near Welwyn Green, and two gates were also placed across the road at the end of Welwyn Lane to the imminent danger of a dire catastrophe through the horses dashing unawares into the obstruction.

These were not the only class of perils to which stage coach travellers were exposed. Disasters often occurred from physical causes, such as stress of weather, snowstorms and other like causes. The year 1836 witnessed one of the most terrific snowstorms about Christmas time, ever experienced. The daily papers of that day record two incidents of the storm in Hertfordshire.

"The Manchester down-mail reached St.

18

Albans, and getting off the road into a hollow, was upset. The guard returned to London in a post chaise and four horses with the bags and passengers."

"About a mile from St. Albans, on the London side, a chariot without horses was seen on Tuesday nearly buried in the snow. There were two ladies inside, who made an earnest appeal to the mail guard, whose coach had got into a drift nearly at the same spot. The ladies said the post-boy had left them to go to St. Albans to get fresh cattle, and had been gone two hours. The guard was unable to assist them, and his mail being extricated, he pursued his journey for London, leaving the chariot and ladies in the situation where they were first seen."

Among the best known coaches were the Red Rover from Manchester, the Defiance, Rocket, Crown, Princes, Regulator, Swallow, Age, Independent, Despatch, Telegraph, Tally Ho, Times, Antelope, and many others. Barnet and St. Albans, and in a lesser degree Hertford, Hatfield, Hitchin and Royston, played an important part in the coaching world, and the large number of old hostelries and posting houses in those towns testify to the large numbers of coaches which used the county's turnpikes. The St. Albans road as far as Hockliffe, below Dunstable, some thirty-six miles from London, was traversed by all the coaches for the north-west and many for the Midlands, and it was at Hockliffe that they took their several ways.

Many of these vehicles kept splendid time, drawing up at their respective places of call with the regularity and punctuality which we now associate with the mail trains. Mr. Ashdown tells us that the Birmingham coach, the Wonder, which left the Peacock at Islington at six o'clock in the morning, covered the distance to St. Albans in two hours. It was indeed the high rate of speed which the mail coaches attained and the punctuality exacted by the postal authorities that led to some of the most serious coaching disasters recorded. An accident to the Liverpool Express just on the county border between Dunstable and St. Albans resulted in the death of one of the passengers. The driver heard the Red Rover from Manchester close behind; he flogged his horses into a gallop and the coach overturned. The two vehicles had reached Daventry in Northamptonshire together and had practically raced all the way to Dunstable. At the trial of the driver at the assizes it was stated that the regulations of the Post Office made it imperative to maintain a uniform of speed of twelve miles an hour.

A race between the Chester mail and the Holyhead mail resulted in a fatal collison at St. Albans in August, 1819. Thomas Perdy and George Butler were indicted for the wilful murder of one of the passengers of the Holyhead mail, of which Perdy was the driver. Both coaches had raced from Highgate and when a mile from St. Albans Perdy put his horses into a furious gallop down the hill. Butler followed his example and endeavoured to overtake the Holyhead coach. "A most terrific race ensued between the coaches, the velocity of both increasing by their own specific gravity down the abrupt hill. The road was wide enough for three coaches to pass each other, but Butler perceiving Perdy was keeping ahead of him pushed his horses on; waving his hat and cheering he suddenly turned his leaders in front of the Holyhead mail, which in consequence being jammed in between the bank of the road and the other vehicle was immediately upset." One man was killed outright and several other passengers suffered most serious iujuries in the frightful impact. The accident happened at eleven o'clock at night and the scene was one of indescribable confusion. In defence of the racing it was urged that by the Post Office regulations the Holyhead mail ought to be at Redbourn, four miles from St. Albans, a quarter of an hour before the other mail.

Through racing and the negligence of the driver, the Fakenham coach was overturned about two miles from Royston, while going down a hill, at seven o'clock in the morning of October 14th, 1825. One of the passengers was very badly injured.

It will not be inappropriate in connection with mail coaching to reproduce the account which the late Mr. Williams tells in his " History of Watford" of the post mistress of that place. He writes :—" The mail bags were conveyed to London by stage coach, and the early coach called at the office for the bags shortly after five o'clock each morning. In response to the thundering knock of the conductor, the old lady left her couch, and thrusting her head, covered with a wide-bordered nightcap, out of the bedroom window, let down the mail bag by a string, and quickly returned to bed again."

An account of the incidents of the road would be sadly incomplete which omitted a mention of the romantic episodes furnished by the youths and maidens, on matrimony intent, bound for the blacksmith's shop at Gretna Green, or the equally accommodating "parson" at Coldstream. The roads from the metropolis to both these hymeneal Meccas led through Hertfordshire, and there are many traditions in the county of post chaises being driven with feverish haste to the north, of angry fathers and guardians in full pursuit, and of the frequent return of the irascible parents with their erring and weeping daughters, whose journey had been cut short before it became too late. The county newspapers for the first few years of the century are full of accounts of fleeing couples and intercepted elopements. Gretna Green being somewhat nearer London was chiefly affected by those intending runaway marriages, and post-masters did a brisk and profitable business in supplying horses for this class of patron.

"Baily's Magazine" records an incident, in 1824, on a Hertford coach of a less romantic and far more gruesome character. One of the passengers was Mary Blanchard, whose husband was lying under sentence of death at Hertford, and she was journeying to the county town to witness the execution. She discovered that her fellow passenger was the Jack Ketch of the period, and in language more forcible than polite, she declared that either she or the hangman must leave the coach. An angry altercation ensued, and matters were becoming serious when the coachman interfered, and Blanchard was put inside. The woman was irrepressible, however, and every now and again put her head out of the window, and roundly abused the executioner.

The effluxions of time and the development of the railways have changed all this. The post chaises and mail coaches have been replaced by the less picturesque and less romantic bicycles, and, to again quote Thackeray, "to those great geniuses now in petticoats who shall write novels for the beloved readers' children, these men and things will be as much legend and history as Nineveh, or Cœur de Lion, or Jack Sheppard. For them stage coaches will have become romances, and a team of four bays as fabulous as Bucephalus or Black Bess."

Index.

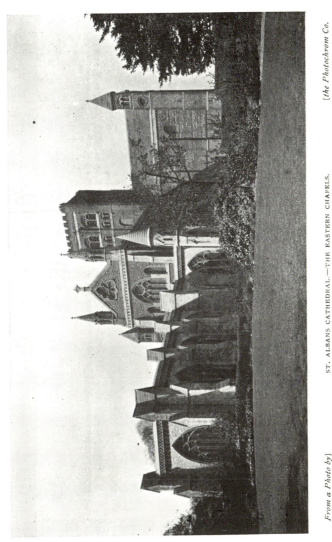

From a Photo by]

ST. ALBANS CATHEDRAL.—THE EASTERN CHAPELS.

[the Photochrom Co.

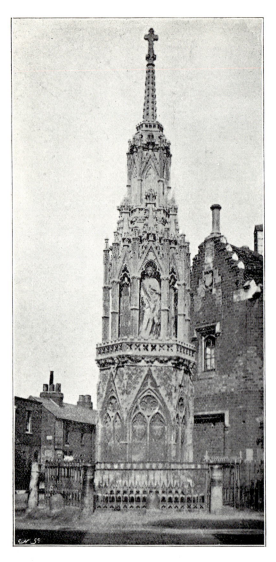

QUEEN ELEANOR MEMORIAL : WALTHAM CROSS
(*before* restoration in 1885-92.)

QUEEN ELEANOR MEMORIAL : WALTHAM CROSS
(*after* restoration in 1885-92.)

MONUMENT TO SIR RALPH SADLEIR, STANDON CHURCH.

From a Photo by A. Whitford Anderson, Esq.]

ANCIENT SCREEN, HITCHIN CHURCH.

[Watford.

PULPIT, ST. MICHAEL'S CHURCH, ST. ALBANS.

LORD BACON'S MONUMENT, ST. MICHAEL'S CHURCH, ST. ALBANS.